# Witchcraft

*(The Big Spell Book)*

*The ultimate guide to witchcraft, spells, rituals and wicca*

## Table of Contents

Introduction

Chapter 1: The History of Witchcraft/ Wicca

Chapter 2: What it Really Means to Be a Witch

Chapter 3: Hedgewitch or Coven?

Chapter 4: Gods That are Honored

Chapter 5: Goddesses That are Honored

Chapter 6: Visualization

Chapter 7: Divination

Chapter 8: Rites and Rituals

Chapter 9: The Sacred Circle and Raising Power

Chapter 10: Spell Casting

Chapter 11: Writing Your Own Spells

Chapter 12: Spells for Attracting Abundance

Chapter 13: Spells for Good Health

Chapter 14: Spells for Attracting Love

Chapter 15: Spells for Good Luck

Conclusion

# Introduction

Every generation seems to search for a new way to do things, a way that is very different to the way of their forefathers. It would seem that today's generation is more and more disillusioned when it comes to organized religion and more likely to look for a less rigid system of beliefs.

We have begun to realize as a community that w have largely lost touch with nature and the natural order that was an important part of daily life in ancient times. More and more people are rediscovering their bond with nature through reverting to the pagan beliefs of the ancients.

More and more we are moving away from a rigid "I am right and you are wrong" belief system to one that is more tolerant. As a result of this new way of thinking, Wicca/ Witchcraft is now one of the fastest growing religions in the world.

The growth of Wicca/ Witchcraft as a religion can, to a large extent, be attributed to the increase amount of information that we have on hand today – today's Wiccans, far from hiding in dark places, can celebrate their religion without fear of being ostracized.

It makes a lot of sense that Wicca has become more popular, considering its focus on working within the natural environment – today's society is one that is very much aware that we need to return to a simpler, more environmentally-friendly way of living.

Is it much surprise then that a religion that celebrates the glories of nature and the natural order has found such a large following in modern society.

For some, there is no other way to survive – if we do not start attuning ourselves to the natural order of things and continue to act in a rigid and intolerant manner, the future looks like a bleak place in deed.

For many, it is the typically intolerant, rigid nature of organized religion that creates disillusionment. Whilst the tenets of most religions preach that love and compassion should be paramount, there is definitely an intolerance that does not gel with these ideals. Christians, for example, are actively encouraged to convert people of other religions.

Today, the words Wicca and Witchcraft are largely interchangeable. It really doesn't matter what you call it, this is a spiritual path of self-growth.

In this book, I am going to introduce to the basic concepts so that you can begin your own spiritual journey and give you the information that you need to make an informed decision about whether or not Wicca is a belief system that resonates with you.

# Chapter 1: The History of Witchcraft/Wicca

## Learn More About the Origins of Witchcraft and Wicca

Witches have never had much of an easy time of things – since ancient times, witchcraft has been associated with evil and malice. In fact, at one time in Ancient Rome, soothsayers – the witches of their day, were banned. In Ancient Egypt, practicing black magic was a crime punishable by death and the pharaoh and priests actively fought the sinister forces and magic in the world.

When Christianity became a universal religion, witches fared no better. In fact, in Christianity, witches are considered hand maidens of the devil. In the Christian bible, it says, "Thou shalt not suffer a witch to live" and this was definitely something that was actively pursued throughout history leading to some of the bloodiest persecution of witches in history.

The Holy Inquisition led a reign of terror from the 14$^{th}$ to 18$^{th}$ centuries, actively looking for witches and eliminating them. Thousands of people died as a result of being accused of witchcraft, many of whom where likely denounced as witches by their enemies and were likely innocent of the charges.

It was a bad time to be a witch – if suspected, you would be tortured until you confessed and then executed. Alternatively, you were given a chance to prove your innocence. One such trial involved being tie to a millstone and throw into a lake. If you floated, it was seen as proof that you were a witch and you'd be executed. If not, you were considered innocent – not much comfort as you would have drowned.

Over time, attitudes began to change when it came to administering torture and to witchcraft itself. Whilst we cannot say that witches have achieved mainstream acceptance across the board, we certainly can say that societal attitudes are changing.

Modern Wicca is said to have started in the 1950's after Britain repealed the Witchcraft Act. After this, practitioners could practice openly without fear of arrest and books on the topic were printed.

Gerald Gardener is by and large considered the father of Wicca because he was one of the first to compile centuries-old information and actual coven practices and publish it in a book. The tradition that he started is known as Gardenerian Wicca and it is still popular to this day.

From the basic principles laid out in the last 60 years, many different traditions have emerged – from those that are super strict in terms of rituals to those who are more relaxed and eclectic.

Fortunately, Wiccans are free to determine what works for them – whilst some covens are really strict, there are others that will allow you to grow in the manner that seems best to you.

# Chapter 2: What it Really Means to Be a Witch

## Being a Witch is About More Than Just Hexes and Magic

Whatever tradition you follow, there are some immutable beliefs that are central to the core of this spiritual system. There is still a lot of leeway for you as a Wiccan to grow and, in essence, the you are left to make your own decisions – there is no divine retribution as such for your actions but you will need to face the consequences of those actions.

## The Wiccan Rede

Alastair Crowley famously said that one of the key beliefs in witchcraft was that you could do whatever you wanted. The Wiccan Rede, however, takes this one step further – you can do whatever you please, as long as you do not cause anyone else harm.

Even when practicing spell-casting, Wiccans are advised to add the clause, "And harm none, so mote it be." Spells can work in weird and wonderful ways – perhaps that prosperity spell will work by letting you win the lotto, perhaps it will mean a loved one dying – not the outcome you would want. Limit any harm in spell-casting by specifically saying that you do not wish to harm anyone.

Foremost among the rules in Wicca, this is one that is not negotiable.

## The Rule of Three

I mentioned above that there is no vengeful deity or divine retribution for you if you commit wrong but that you do have to face the consequences of what you do. So what stops a Wiccan from cursing people then?

For starters, the Wiccan Rede states that you can do whatever you want, as long as you do not harm anyone.

Secondly, we have the Rule of Three – quite simply, what you give out, you get back three times over. So curse your boss at work if you really want to, just be prepared to accept that the same negative energy will be coming back at you three times over and will hit you hard.

It is kind of like the concept of Karma, except that you will reap whatever you sow in this lifetime – it won't necessarily be carried forward to the next one.

## We Are the World

Everyone and everything is inter-connected. By helping one person, you can make the world a better place. Everything that you do has an impact on someone else so it is important to always try to act for the good.

## Nature is Key

Wiccans understand the importance of nature and the natural order of things. In some traditions, the divine is accessed through nature and so it is really important to work with nature, rather than against it.

Spells are made more powerful by timing them correctly in terms of the stages of the moon and natural talismans, etc. are afforded a special place in magic working.

## Sorry, No Satan

Wiccans take complete responsibility for everything that they do. Wiccans do not believe in the concept of an evil devil who leads you astray. There is no Wiccan hell.

Understanding this can be both empowering and frightening – knowing that you are in complete control of your actions opens your eyes to a world of possibilities but also stops you being able to blame others for your actions.

## No One Religion is the Only Spiritual Path

This is a concept that may be difficult for our egos to accept but if you truly want to follow the Wiccan path, you need to accept that there are many different spiritual paths that can be followed successfully.

Whilst you may disagree with your neighbor's belief system, you do have to accept that it may also be a valid one. There is no right and wrong belief in Wicca – Wiccans are, by nature a very tolerant people.

# Chapter 3: Hedgewitch or Coven?

## Should You Practice Your Craft Alone?

In the past, hedgewitches would live on the outskirts of villages and provide spells and natural medicines to local townsfolk. A hedgewitch is the name now most commonly applied to a solo practitioner.

Whether or not you choose to join a coven is going to depend on where you live and what your own personal preferences are. There are advantages and disadvantages to each path.

## Solo Practitioner

Being a solo practitioner does afford you a lot more freedom when it comes to following your own path. Many covens have a degree system that new members need to work through in order to progress and you may find that, for you, progressing in this manner is too slow.

Perhaps you prefer being on your own or you are not into all the rituals that covens typically follow. Being a solo practitioner allows for a more eclectic spiritual path.

That said, it can be a lonely road – you will not have the support of a coven to sustain you and will not be able to draw on the experience of fellow witches in your area.

## Joining a Coven

The primary problem when it comes to joining a coven may be a geographical one. Are there covens in your area? If so, do you know how to find them? If not, you may not have the option of joining a coven at all.

If there is a coven in your area, you may even find that there is a problem getting into it – some covens are close-knit groups that won't easily admit new members.

If you crave a more structured approach to learning about Wicca, you might find that in a coven.

A coven will also provide fellowship and support for you – you will always have someone to support you in your own journey and people who can share their experiences with you.

Like with any other group, you do want to ensure that you and the coven share the same values – you should feel comfortable in the group.

## A Compromise Might Work

You will find that there are several online communities and forums that you are able to join up with and this could provide a suitable compromise – offering you the benefit of being supported by a community and their experiences whilst also allowing you the freedom to do your own thing.

# Chapter 4: Gods That are Honored

## Gods Honored Throughout History That May Resonate With You

This is another area where beginners may become a little confused. There are several paths that you can follow when it comes to choosing which Gods to worship. What follows is a list of the major Gods worshipped across time. I have divided them into the cultures that they originate from. Read through these lists and find the Gods that resonate with you on a personal level.

As a Wicca, you do not need to be restricted to one particular tradition and can pick and choose Gods from across the cultures. You can choose a particular God with the powers that match your spell. The Gods and Goddesses do not mind being called upon to help – even if you do not normally worship them, as long as you show the proper respect.

In order to find out who your patron deities are, it is useful to meditate on the subject – they will soon make themselves known to you.

You will find that there is often some overlap in different cultures – this is because many traditions adopted the basics beliefs of those that went before. In many cases, one God or Goddess will simply be a different facet of another.

Wiccans believe that the Gods and Goddesses are benevolent beings and they are viewed with reverence, though more as friends than anything else.

## The Horned God

This is more a representation of the male side of divine nature and the Horned God has been revered for centuries as the representation of nature itself.

## Egyptian

**Amun /Amen /Ammon:** God of reproduction, fertility, agriculture, prophecy. Associated with the ram and the goose.

**Anubis:** God of death, endings, wisdom, surgery, hospital stays, finding lost things, journeys, and protection. Considered a messenger from the gods to humans, he was associated with the jackal and sometimes the dog.

**Horus:** God of the sun and the moon, and son of Isis and Osiris, he stands for prophecy, justice, success and problem solving. He tried to avenge his father's murder and lost an eye for the trouble. Associated with the falcon and the hawk.

**Imhotep:** God of medicine and healing.

**Osiris:** The supreme Egyptian god. Fertility, civilization, agriculture, crafts, judgment, architecture, social laws, power, growth, and stability. Associated with the hawk and the phoenix.

**Ptah:** God of artisans and artists, builders and craftsmen. Associated with the bull.

**Thoth:** God of books and learning, and the greatest of magicians. Writing, inventions, the arts, divination, commerce, healing, intuition, success, wisdom, truth, and the Akashic Records. Associated with the ibis.

## Middle Eastern

**Addad:** Canaan, Babylon, Assyria, Syria, Mesopotamia. God of storms, earthquakes, floods, and furious winds. Associated with lightning and the bull.

**Adonis:** Semitic god. Harvest, death, and resurrection. Associated with the boar.

**Ahura Mazdah:** Persia and Zoroastrianism. God of universal law, purification, and goodness. One of his symbols was the winged disk.

**Asshur:** Assyria, Babylon. Supreme god represented by a winged disk. Fertility, protection, victory, and bravery. Associated with the bull.

**Dumuzi/ Tammuz:** Mesopotamia, Sumeria. Called the Anointed God. Harvest and fertility.

**Ea/ Enki:** Mesopotamia, Babylon, Sumeria. Creator god of carpenters, stonecutters, and goldsmiths; patron of all the arts. Associated with the goat, the fish, the eye, and the vase.

**Enlil/ Bel:** Sumeria, Babylon, Assyria. King of the gods. Destructive winds, hurricanes, floods, storms, and the laws.

**Marduk:** God of fate, courage, healing, justice, the law, and victory. Associated with the bull.

**Mithra/ Mithras:** Persia; god of many Middle Eastern cultures. The sun, warriors, contracts, predictions, wisdom, sacred oaths, prosperity, and spiritual illumination. Associated with the disk or circle and the cave.

**Shamash/ Chemosh**: Mesopotamia, Sumeria, Babylon, Assyria. God of the sun, divination, retribution, courage, triumph, and justice.

**Sin** Mesopotamia, Ur, Assyria, Babylon, Sumeria. God of the moon, the calendar, destiny, predictions, and secrets. Associated with lapis lazuli and the dragon.

## Greek

**Apollo:** God of the light of the sun, healing, oracles, poetry, music, inspiration, magick, and the arts. Associated with the arrow, bay laurel, and the raven.

**Ares:** God of war, terror, courage, raw energy, and stamina.

**Helios:** God of the actual sun, riches, and enlightenment.

**Hephaestus:** God of blacksmiths, metalworkers, craftsmen, and volcanoes. Associated with pottery.

**Hermes:** Messenger of the Gods. Commerce, good luck, orthodox medicine, occult wisdom, music, merchants, and diplomacy. Associated with the ram.

**Pan:** God of male sexuality, animals, fertility, farming, medicine, and soothsaying. Associated with goats, fish, and bees.

**Poseidon:** God of the seas and all sea animals. Storms, hurricanes, earthquakes, horses, rain, human emotions, sailors, and weather. Associated with the horse, fish, dolphin, and bull.

**Zeus:** God of the Heavens. Rain, storms, lightning, wisdom, justice, the law, riches, and the heart's desires. Associated with the eagle, oak, and lightning.

## Roman

**Bacchus/ Liber:** God of good times, wine, and fertility. Associated with the goat and vine.

**Faunus/ Lupercus:** God of nature and woodlands. Farming, music, dance, and agriculture. Associated with the goat, bees, and fish.

**Janus:** God of two faces representing the past and the future. Beginnings and endings, new cycles, and journeys. Associated with doors.

**Jupiter:** King of Heaven. Storms, rain, honor, riches, friendships, the heart's desires, and protection. Associated with lightning.

**Mars:** God of war, terror, revenge, and courage. Associated with the woodpecker, horse, wolf, oaks, and laurel.

**Mercury:** Messenger of the Gods. God of commerce, cunning, success, magick, travel, and merchants. Associated with the caduceus.

**Neptune:** Sea god of earthquakes, storms, ships, the seas, and horses. Also associated with the bull and the dolphin.

**Saturn:** God of abundance, prosperity, and karmic lessons. Associated with the sickle, corn, and the vine.

## African

**Asa:** Kenya. God of mercy, surviving the impossible or insurmountable.

**Fa Dahomey:** God of personal destiny.

**Famian:** Guinea. God of fertility and protector against demons.

**Katonda:** East Africa. God of judgment, and against all odds, and divination.

**Mukuru:** Southwest Africa. God of rain, healing, and protection.

**Mungo:** Kenya. God of rain.

**Nyame:** West Africa. God who prepared the soul for rebirth.

**Ogijn:** West Africa. God of iron and warfare, removal of difficulties, and justice.

**Olorun:** Yoruba. God of truth, foreseeing, and victory against odds.

**Shango:** Nigeria. God of storm and war.

**Wele:** Bantu. God of rain, storms, creativity, and prosperity.

## Celtic

**Angus Mac Og:** Ireland. God of love. Associated with birds.

**Bel:** Ireland. God of the sun, healing, science, success, and prosperity.

**Bran:** Wales. God of prophecy, the arts, leadership, music, and writing. Associated with the raven.

**Cernunnos:** Known to all Celt areas. God of the woodlands and wild animals. Fertility, physical love, reincarnation, and wealth. Associated with the serpent, stag, ram, and bull.

**The Dagda:** Ireland. High King of the Tuatha De Danann, the ancient Irish deities. Patron of priests; the arts, prophecy, weather, reincarnations, knowledge, healing, and prosperity.

**Diancecht:** Ireland. God of healing, medicine, and regeneration. Associated with herbs and the snake.

**Lugh:** Ireland, Wales. God of crafts, the arts, magick, journeys, healing, initiation, and prophecy. Associated with the raven, stag, and dog.

**Manannan Mac Lir/ Manawrydan Ap Llyr:** Ireland, Wales. God of magick, storms, sailors, weather forecasting, merchants, and commerce. Associated with the pig, apple, and cauldron.

**Ogma:** Ireland. God of poets and writers, physical strength, inspiration, and magick.

## Norse

**Aegir:** God of the sea, brewing, prosperity, sailors, and weather.

**Baldur/ Balder:** God of the sun, reconciliation, gentleness, reincarnation, and harmony.

**Freyr/ Frey:** The god of Yule. God of fertility, love, abundance, horses, sailors, happiness, and weather. Associated with the boar.

**Heimdall:** God of the rainbow, beginnings and endings, and defense against evil. Associated with the bridge.

**Loki:** A trickster and shapechanger. God of earthquakes, fire, cunning, deceit, daring, and revenge. Associated with the wolf and snake.

**Njord:** God of the sea, fishing, sailors, prosperity, and journeys.

**Odin:** King of the Gods. God of runes, poetry, magick, divination, storms, rebirth, knowledge, weather, justice, and inspiration. Associated with the wolf and raven.

**Thor:** Protector of the common person. God of thunder, storms, law and order, strength, weather, and trading voyages. Associated with the goat, oak, and lightning.

**Tyr:** The bravest of the gods. God of victory, justice, the law, honor, and athletes.

## Russian-Slovenian

**Dazhbog:** God of the sun, fair judgment, and destiny.

**Perun:** God of storms, purification, fertility, oracles, defense against illness, victory, and oak forests. Associated with the cock, goat, bear, bull, and lightning.

**Scantovit:** Four-headed god of divination, prosperity, victory, and battles. Associated with the horse.

## Indian

**Agni:** God of fire, rain, storms, protector of the home, new beginnings, and justice.

**Brahma:** God of creation and wisdom; often portrayed as having four heads, each facing different directions. Associated with the swan.

**Buddha:** The Enlightened One, the Awakened One, the Way-Shower.

**Chandra/ Soma:** Moon god of psychic visions and dreams.

**Ganesha:** Elephant-headed god of beginnings, writing, worldly success, learning, prosperity, journeys, and overcoming obstacles. Associated with the elephant and flowers.

**Indra:** King of the Gods. God of fertility, reincarnation, rain, the rainbow, the law, opposition to evil, creativity, and the sun. Associated with the elephant, horse, dog, and lightning.

**Krishna:** God of erotic delights and music, and savior from sin. Associated with the star.

**Shiva:** Demon-Slayer. He is shown with a third eye in the center of his forehead and four arms. God of fertility, physical love, medicine, storms, long life, healing, righteousness, and judgment. Associated with cattle, the bull, elephant, serpent, lightning, and the hourglass.

**Vishnu:** God of peace, power, compassion, abundance, and success. Associated with the lotus, serpent, and shells.

## Chinese

**Erh-Iang:** God of protection from evil.

**Fu-Hsi:** God of happiness, destiny, and success. Associated with the hat.

**Hsuan-T'ien-Shang-Ti:** God of exorcism of evil spirits.

**K'Uei-Hsing:** God of tests and examinations, protector of travelers.

**Lei-King:** God who punished the guilty that human laws did not touch.

**Lu-Hsing:** God of salaries and employees. Associated with deer.

**Shen Nung:** God of medicine.

**Shou-Hsing:** God of longevity and old people. Associated with the peach.

**T'ai-Yueh-Ta-Ti:** God of fortune, payment of karmic debt, and prosperity.

**Tsai Shen:** God of wealth. Associated with the carp and cock.

**Tsao Wang:** God of the hearth and kitchen. He is said to guard the hearth and family, allotting next year's fortune.

**Twen-Chang:** God of literature and poetry.

**Yao-Shih:** Master of healing and psychic abilities.

## Japanese

**Bishamonten:** God of happiness.

**Daikoku:** God of prosperity.

**Ebisu:** God of work.

**Fukurokuju:** God of happiness and long life.

**Hotei Osho:** God of good fortune.

**Jurojin:** God of happiness and long life.

## North American

**Agloolik:** Eskimo. God of hunters and fishermen.

**Ioshekha:** Iroquois/Heron. God who defeats demons and heals diseases.

**Tirawa:** Pawnee. God of hunting, agriculture, and religious rituals.

**Wakonda:** Lakota. God of all wisdom and power.

**Yanauluha:** Zuni. The great medicine god. Civilization, animal husbandry, healing, and knowledge.

## Mayan

**Hurukan:** God of fire, the whirlwind, hurricanes, and spiritual illumination.

**Itzamna:** God of knowledge, writing, fertility, regeneration, and medicine. Associated with the lizard.

**Kukulcan:** God of learning, culture, the laws, and the calendar.

**Yum Caax:** God of maize, fertility, riches, and life.

## Aztec

**Itzcolihuqhui:** God of darkness, volcanic eruptions, and disaster. Associated with obsidian.

**Quetzalcoatl:** God of wind, life breath, civilization, the arts, and fate.

**Tlaloc:** God of thunder, rain, fertility, and water. Associated with lightning and the pitcher or vase.

## Incan

**Inti:** Sun god of fertility and crops. Associated with corn.

**Pachacamac:** God of the arts and occupations, and oracles.

**Viracocha:** God of the arts, the sun, storms, oracles, moral codes, and rain.

# Chapter 5: Goddesses That are Honored

## Goddesses Honored Throughout the Ages That May Resonate With You

Once again, call on the Goddesses that you can most identify with, or the ones that you need to ask to bless a particular spell.

## The Triple Goddess of the Moon

Many Wiccans recognize the Triple Goddess of the Moon as the true goddess and worship her in her varying forms of Maiden, Mother and Crone. She is seen as the embodiment of life itself and the progression of time.

## Eygptian

**Bast:** The cat-headed goddess of all animals, but especially cats. She symbolizes the moon, childbirth, fertility, pleasure, joy, music, dance, marriage, and healing.

**Buto:** Cobra goddess of protection.

**Hathor:** A mother and creator goddess, protector of women. Symbols include the moon, marriage, motherhood, artists, music, happiness, and prosperity. She is associated with the cow, the frog, and the cat.

**Isis:** The supreme Egyptian goddess, who was honored for 3,000 years. In later times, her worship spread to Greece and Rome. Meanings include magick, fertility, marriage, purification, initiation, reincarnation, healing, divination, the arts, and protection. Associated with the cat, the goose, and the cow.

**Maat:** Goddess of judgment, truth, justice, and reincarnation. Associated with ostrich feathers.

**Neith:** A warrior goddess and protectress, she represents magick, healing, mystical knowledge, domestic arts, and marriage. Two arrows were among her symbols. She was associated with the vulture.

**Nepthys:** The dark sister of Isis. Magick, protection, dreams, and intuition. The basket was one of her symbols.

**Sekhmet:** The dark sister of Bast, a lion-headed goddess. Physicians and bonesetters; revenge, and power. Both revered and feared – offerings were given to appease her as much to ask for her favor. She was once tasked with the destruction of mankind but Ra changed his mind and sent Hathor to stop her. This was done by giving her a draft of beer that made her sleepy and so mankind was saved. Associated with the lioness.

**Tauret:** The hippopotamus goddess. Childbirth, maternity, and protection.

## Middle East

**Astarte:** Known as Ashtart in Phoenicia. Queen of Heaven. The moon, astrology, victory, revenge, and sexual love. Among her symbols were the eight-pointed star and the crescent.

**Inanna:** Canaan, Phoenicia, Sumeria, Uruk, Babylon. Queen of the Heavens. Defense, victory, love, fertility, destiny, prosperity, and justice. Associated with the star, the serpent staff, and dogs.

**Ishtar:** Lady of Heaven. Patroness of priestesses; sexual love, fertility, revenge, resurrection, marriage, initiation, overcoming obstacles, and social laws. Associated with the lion, the serpent staff, the dragon, the eight-pointed star, the dove, the double ax, the rainbow, and the bridge. She had a rainbow necklace similar that that of the Norse god Freyja.

**Lilith:** Protectress of all pregnant women, mothers, and children. Associated with the owl.

**Mari/ Meri/ Marratu:** Syria, Chaldea, Persia. Goddess of fertility, childbirth, the moon, and the sea. One of her symbols was the pearl.

**Tiamat:** Mesopotamia, Babylon, Sumeria. Goddess of destruction, karmic discipline, death, and regeneration. Associated with the dragon and the serpent.

## Greek

**Aphrodite:** Goddess of love, sensuality, passion, partnerships, fertility, renewal, the sea, joy, and beauty. Associated with the swan, dove, poppy, rose, apple, and pomegranate.

**Artemis:** Virgin Huntress. Goddess of wild places and wild animals, protectress of young girls. Magick, psychic power, fertility, childbirth, sports, contact with nature, and mental healing. Associated with dogs, the stag, horse, acorn, crescent, and juniper.

**Athena:** Goddess of Athens. Freedom and women's rights; patroness of career women; patroness of craftsmen. Wisdom, justice, writing, music, the sciences, invention, weaving, architects, and renewal. Associated with the owl, horse, intertwined snakes, the olive, and oak.

**Cybele:** A Phrygian Great Mother goddess of the earth and caverns, associated with the god Attis. Goddess of the natural world and wild beasts. The moon, magick, wildlife, and the dead. Originally worshipped in the form of a black meteorite, Cybele's worship spread to ancient Greece and Rome. Associated with the lion, bees, pomegranate, violets, pine, cypress, the cave, bowl, and pearl.

**Demeter:** Goddess of the Eleusinian Mysteries. Protector of women; crops, initiation, renewal, fertility, civilization, the law, motherhood, and marriage. Associated with corn and wheat.

**Gaea/Gaia:** Earth Goddess. Oaths, divination, healing, motherhood, marriage, and dreams. The Oracle at Delphi was originally hers, before Apollo took over. Associated with the laurel.

**Hades:** God of the Underworld. Elimination of fear of the dead. Associated with gemstones.

**Hecate:** A Thracian Triple Goddess of the moon and the Underworld with great power. Patroness of priestesses. The moon, prophecy, averting evil, riches, victory, travelers, crossroads, transformation, purification, and renewal. Associated with the snake, dragon, dogs, and cauldron.

**Hera:** Queen of the Gods. Use her image when facing infidelity and insecurity, and also for marriage and childbirth. Associated with the peacock, cow, pomegranate, marjoram, lily, apple, flowers, willow, the sickle, and double ax.

**Hestia:** Virgin Goddess of the hearth. The home, dedication to duty, and discipline. Her name was mentioned by the Greeks in all their prayers and sacrifices.

**Nike:** Goddess of victory. Associated with the palm branch.

**Persephone:** Queen of the Underworld. The seasons, crops, and overcoming obstacles. Associated with the bat, willow, narcissus, pomegranate, sheaf, corn, and cornucopia. She was so beautiful that she was kidnapped by Hades and taken to the underworld. Her mother, Ceres petitioned for her release and this was granted on condition that she spend time in the underworld. As she had eaten seeds when in the underworld, she was to stay there for 6 months of the year. It was said to be because Ceres missed her daughter so much during these 6 months that winter came about.

**Hemis:** Goddess of law and order. Associated with the scales.

**Ceres:** The Grain Goddess. Crops, initiation, protector of women, and motherhood. Associated with corn and wheat.

**Diana:** Goddess of the woodlands and wild animals, childbirth and women. Associated with deer, dogs, and the stag.

**Fortuna:** Goddess of fate, oracles, and chance. Associated with the wheel and cornucopia.

**Juno:** Queen of Heaven. Women's fertility, childbirth, the home, and marriage. Associated with the peacock, goose, and the veil.

**Minerva:** Goddess of women's rights and freedom. Artisans, craftsmen, renewal, and protection. Associated with spinning and weaving, the owl, horse, snake, spear, and pillar.

**Venus:** Goddess of love, fertility, and renewal. Also associated with the dove.

## African

**Ala/ Ale:** Nigeria. Earth Mother and creator goddess. Community laws, morality, and oaths.

**Mbaba Mwana Waresa:** Zulu. Goddess of the rainbow and crops.

**Rubanga:** Banyoro. God of fertility, children, harvest, health, and rebirth.

**Yemaya:** Yoruba. Goddess of women and children.

# Celtic

**Anu:** Ireland. Goddess of fertility, prosperity, and health. Associated with cows.

**Arianrhod:** Wales. Goddess of beauty and reincarnation. Associated with the wheel.

**Badb:** Ireland. Goddess of wisdom, inspiration, and enlightenment. Associated with the cauldron, crow, and raven.

**Blodeuwed:** Wales. Goddess of wisdom, lunar mysteries, and initiation. Associated with flowers and the owl.

**Branwyn:** Wales. Goddess of love and beauty. Associated with the cauldron.

**Brigit/ Brigid:** Ireland. Goddess of all feminine arts and crafts. Healing, inspiration, learning, poetry, divination, and occult knowledge. Associated with weaving.

**Cerridwen:** Wales. Goddess of regeneration, initiation, inspiration, magick, poetry, and knowledge. Associated with the cauldron and the sow.

**Danu:** Ireland. Goddess of prosperity, magick, and wisdom.

**Epona:** Britain, Gaul. Goddess of horses, dogs, and prosperity.

**Macha:** Ireland. Goddess of war, cunning, sexuality, and dominance over males. Associated with the raven and the crow.

**Morrigan:** Ireland, Wales. Patroness of priestesses. Goddess of revenge, magick, and prophecy. Associated with the crow and raven.

**Scathach/ Scota:** Ireland, Scotland. Goddess of martial arts, blacksmiths, prophecy, and magick.

## Norse

**Audhumla:** Goddess of motherhood, child-rearing, and home crafts. Associated with the cow.

**Freya:** Mistress of cats and a shapeshifter. Goddess of love, sex, childbirth, enchantments, wealth, trance, wisdom, good luck, fertility, writing, and protection. Associated with the horse, cat, and amber.

**Hel:** Queen of the Underworld. Revenge, fate, and karma.

**Idunn/ Idun:** Goddess of immortality, youth, and long life. Associated with the apple.

## Russian/ Slovenian

**Baba Yaga:** Goddess of endings, death, and revenge. Associated with the snake.

**Diiwica:** Goddess of the hunt and the forests, hounds, victory, and success. Associated with the horse and dog.

**Dzidzileyla/ Didilia:** Goddess of marriage, fertility, and love.

**Mati Syra Zemlya:** Goddess of the earth, crops, fertility, oaths, justice, divination, and property disputes.

**Durga:** Goddess of nurturing, protection, and defense. Associated with the lion and bowl.

**Kali/ Kali Ma:** Goddess of Death. Goddess of regeneration, sexual love, and revenge; protectress of women. Associated with the wheel, knot, braid, and snake.

**Lakshmi:** Goddess of love, beauty, creative energy, agriculture, good fortune, prosperity, and success.

**Sarasvati:** Goddess of the creative arts, science, and teaching. Associated with the lotus and crescent.

**Tara:** Goddess of spiritual enlightenment, knowledge, and compassion. In Tibet, Tara has twenty-one forms and colors; the most familiar forms being the Green Tara for growth and protection, and the White Tara for long life, health, and prosperity.

## Chinese

**Chuang Mu:** Goddess of the bedroom and sexual delights.

**Kuan Yin:** Goddess of fertility, children, motherhood, childbirth, and mercy. She is often portrayed holding a child in one arm and a willow twig or lotus blossom in her other hand. Associated with the willow.

## Japanese

**Amaterasu:** Sun goddess of harvest, fertility, and light. Associated with weaving.

**Benten:** Goddess of good luck and protection from earthquakes.

**Benzaiten:** Goddess of love.

**Inari:** Fox-goddess of merchants, business, and prosperity. Associated with the fox and rice.

**Jizo Bosatsu:** Protector of women in childbirth, and children.

**Kishmojin:** Goddess of children, compassion, and fertility.

## North America

**Ataentsic:** Iroquois/Heron. Goddess of marriage and childbirth.

**Onatha:** Iroquois. Goddess of wheat and harvest.

**Spider Woman:** Navajo. Goddess of charms and magick.

**Ixchel:** Goddess of childbirth, medicine, pregnancy, and domestic arts, especially weaving.

## Aztec

**Chalchiuitlicue:** Goddess of storms, whirlpools, love, and flowers.

**Chantico:** Goddess of the home, fertility, and wealth. Associated with snakes and gemstones.

**Coatlicue:** Goddess of famines and earthquakes. Associated with snakes.

**Itzpaplotl:** Goddess of fate and agriculture.

**Mayauel:** Goddess of childbirth. Associated with the bowl, turtle, and snake.

**Tozi:** Goddess of midwives, healers, and healing.

# Inca

**Chasca:** Goddess of girls and flowers.

**Mama Quilla:** Goddess of married women and the calendar.

# Chapter 6: Visualizati(

## The Power of Visualization  Divine

Meditation and visualization techniqu(
connect with the divine mind. It is a w
deity and identifying who that deity actu

## How To Begin All Visualiza

Slow your breathing and aim for steady deep breathing, rather than shallow quick breathing. Take a deep breath and relax all the muscles in your body. Take another deep breath and relax your mind; think of a place that you love and that has positive associations for you. Take another deep breath and imagine you are floating freely in a a calm, safe environment. Continue until you are completely relaxed and calm.

Once this is done, you are ready to start raise your personal energy. As you count down from ten slowly, imagine pulling in energy deep into your navel and that it is ready for use.

When you reach one, you will be ready to start your visualization.

## Your Patron Deity

Finding your patron deity could involve expending a bit of effort but the really good news is that you are bound to know them when you do find them. Meditating on who you patron deity is invites them to make themselves known to you.

Start your visualization by seeing a large door in your minds eye. Step through the door and note what images are shown to you. Are you in a forest, near water, in a field? You will be in a place that is sacred to your patron deity and this will be your first clue.

Wander through this world slowly, taking note of the sights, sounds and anything that draws your attention.

...sualization, you will often find that your patron deity gives ... to who they are. They can do this by showing you themselves, ...ifts for you and possibly even telling you who they are.

... the visualization is over, look out for little signs in the real world to ...ow you that your patron deity is around.

Alternatively, choose your deity in accordance with your needs at the moment. Let's say that you want your family to be safe, Vesta, Goddess of the Hearth, might resonate with you. It may seem at odds with our upbringing to pick and choose in this manner but this is what was done by many of the ancients.

Ancient Romans, for example, believed that there was a God/ Goddess in everything and that could help you with just about everything you needed help with. You would make your offering to the God/ Goddess that you needed help from and, when you no longer needed them, thanked them and moved on.

After having read the previous two chapters, you will be more familiar with the various pantheons of Gods and Goddesses. Some of those names might have jumped out at you and felt familiar. Go with these instincts as these are bound to be deities with whom you have had a previous connection in the past.

Some names mean more to you than others do. Some may even feel like old friends. Finding your patron deity is like coming home to a good friend.

And remember, Wicca can be eclectic, you can resonate with Gods and Goddesses from different eras and even from different pantheons.

## Visualization in Spell-Casting

When casting spells, you need to visualize your outcome. This helps to prevent there being any confusion as to what you are hoping to achieve. Really take the time to visualize your desired outcome and make it as real as possible in your mind's eye.

How would you feel if your spell worked? What would you do differently? All of these emotions can help to create a much more realistic visualization.

# Chapter 7: Divination

## Finding Out What the Future Holds

There are a number of different divination techniques – you will need to decide which works best for you as a whole. Some are easier than others, some, like pendulum divination are best suited for yes/no answers. Others, like tarot cards are more suited to longer answers and are more open to interpretation.

## Learning to Read Tarot Cards

Tarot cards can be another useful tool for the more advanced Wiccan. Bear in mind that the cards are largely open to personal interpretation and are more suited to providing general insights than Yes or No answers.

Reading the cards involves also drawing on your own intuition as a Wiccan and so two readings by two different people can be different.

It is important to learn more about how to read the cards before performing readings for other people - it can take a lifetime to learn how to properly interpret the cards.

The interpretation of the cards is also only part of it - you also need to learn what the different spreads are and which spreads to use in which occasions.

With tarot cards, it is better that you are the main person to handle your own deck. If you are doing a reading for someone else, you can ask them to shuffle the pack once or twice. Whilst shuffling the pack, the question that is to be asked should be held in mind.

The cards that are drawn, in addition to whether the picture lies upside down or not can also make a difference when it comes to the interpretation of the cards.

Typically, when a card is drawn and the picture lies upside down, the meaning of the card is reversed as well.

As you progress along your journey, you will learn how to interpret the cards properly.

Some people are not comfortable with tarot cards and, of you fall into this category, do not be concerned - as always, the choice is yours whether to follow this particular path or not.

## Oracle Cards

Oracle cards are less intimidating for the beginner and can allow you insight – the Gods and Goddesses can still send messages through these cards. These work in much the same way as tarot cards do but each card will provide you with a specific message or lesson that you need to take note of.

Once again, hold the question that you want answered in mind whilst shuffling the cards and ask for guidance.

## Scrying

Scrying is a useful tool for those looking for waking insights. Scrying basically means "to discern" and involves achieving an altered state of conscious through concentrating on an item. This can be a mirror, a crystal ball, a flame or even a bowl of water.

Stare into the ball or item, keeping the question you want answers to in mind, until you see nothing else in the room but the item. The actual form the answers will take will depend on you personally but will often be a series of fleeting thoughts or feelings that you will need to make sense of.

## Pendulum Divination

This is one of the oldest and most simple forms of divination. All you need is a balanced weight on the end of a string or chain. You can even, if you want to, use a necklace. Some people use a ring placed on a chain – the key is to ensure that the weight is evenly balanced so that it works well.

Start by holding the end of the chain in your dominant hand. Your other palm should be face up, about an inch or two below the end of the chain. Clear your mind and hold the pendulum steady.

Now think "Yes". The pendulum will either sway back and forth or move in a circle. Note what it does.

Now think "No". The pendulum should move differently now. If "Yes" made it sway back and forth, "No" will make it move in circles. Conversely, if "Yes" made it move in a circular motion, "No" will move it back and forth.

The action will be different for most people and so you need to establish which direction signifies "Yes" and which direction signifies "No".

Retest by repeating "Yes" and "No" just to be sure and then you can concentrate on asking your question.

As mentioned above, this method is best suited to questions that require simple "Yes" or "No" answers.

Every time you use the pendulum in future, repeat the test for "Yes" and "No" again, to confirm the directions again.

## Palm Reading

Palm reading is again more about interpretation rather than strictly a set of rules. The palm of your dominant hand points to the life you have been dealt now and can change over time. The palm of the other hand shows the potential that you were born with. Look closely and you will pick up differences between the two.

## Analyzing Dreams

Dreaming has long been held to be an important way for the subconscious mind to process the events of the day and to consolidate memories and facilitate learning. Dreaming can also have spiritual significance. The Gods and Goddesses can also communicate with us when we dream so dreams can be an important way to divine what their plans are for us.

There are many different beliefs out there on what happens when we dream - some cultures believe that dreaming allows us entrance to the astral plane, others that it allows us to commune with the spirit world, others that it allows us to access knowledge from deep within our subconscious minds.

Whatever system of beliefs you subscribe to, dream-work can be a useful exercise but it should be noted that you need to regularly record your dreams so that you can notice patterns that emerge.

Start by keeping a notebook and pen next to your bed. Record what you remember about your dream as soon as you wake up. Don't bother with prose here, note down key words and feelings - dreams are very fleeting and you won't remember them for long.

An interesting exercise is to write down just three of four words that will help you to remember your dream later, as soon as you wake up. Carry on doing this for at least a week, until it becomes habit.

Much of what we do as Wiccans is bound to natural cycles so it is also important to record the phase of the moon alongside the words you have recorded. You are bound to find that your dreams are tied into the lunar cycle - being more easily interpreted and useful during some phases of the moon than during others.

Interpreting the messages within the dream becomes easier the longer you carry on with it. You may find it helpful to consult a dream dictionary but it is more important to study the dream in the context of your own life experience - dream dictionaries offer very general interpretations.

Look for evidence of issues that you have been wrestling with - dreams will often be very symbolic in nature so the meaning won't be immediately clear but something should make sense to you after a while. Analyzing your dreams can be a wonderful tool for personal growth.

If there is something in particular that you want to know, or if you are looking for clarification, spend a little time thinking about this issue just before going to sleep - your subconscious mind should provide answers for you.

# Chapter 8: Rites and Rituals

## Preparing for Sacred Rites and Rituals

Preparing yourself for rites and rituals means that you will need to have a sacred space that you can go to. Whilst any place can be considered sacred, having a dedicated space with an altar will help you to focus your energies correctly.

This will be your special place to commune with your patron deities on a daily basis and where you can perform spells and honor your deities.

Your altar can be made up of anything that you want and you can use whatever feels right to you to set it up. It can be indoors or outdoors, large or small – depending on your needs.

Decorating the altar with symbols helps to personalize it and choosing symbols that are meaningful to you can go a long way to helping you focus your energies.

## Choosing Altar Symbols

You may wish to have all Goddess statues, or you may choose to have both God and Goddess images. Perhaps you will prefer no images at all. Every altar will reflect the personality and spirituality of the person who erects it.

Using the four elements on an altar will bring the energies associated with these elements to your sacred space. Fire can be a candle; Air, incense; Earth, a stone or flowers; Water, a fountain or water in a vase.

Or each of these elements might be portrayed in a picture that speaks to you. By placing the elements on your altar, you are subconsciously asking that balance come to your space and life.

Certain flowers and the wood of trees have traditional meanings and can be used to symbolize specific energies. So can objects, such as a pyramid, box, animal figurine, or stone.

Or you may decide to incorporate images and objects that remind you of a person you wish to remember or an event or action you desire to accomplish.

Listen with your gut, and choose what feels right to you.

If you burn candles on your altar, be certain that the candle is firmly set in a metal holder and is well away from anything flammable. The last thing you want is a devastating fire ruining your home.

Incense is also a potential problem if not handled with care. Stick incense should be placed in a can of sand or a holder large enough not to tip over. Cone incense should be placed in an unbreakable, heat-resistant holder or on a bed of sand. If you burn paper requests at your altar, use a metal bowl or cauldron.

## Symbols and Sacred Objects

Throughout the centuries, humans have used many different symbols and objects as part of their individual and collective spiritual worship. Since the collective unconscious mind of every human, as described by Carl Jung, is connected to the symbols used by our ancestors through genetic memory, these objects and symbols still have deep meaning for us.

The subconscious mind does not speak in words, but only in nonverbal symbols. By using symbolic objects on your altars, you are communicating with your subconscious mind, the conduit through which flow psychic messages, spiritual communications, and extrasensory perception, all the little nudges and gut feelings that help us deal with life's difficulties.

To open the door to the collective unconscious, one must enter through the subconscious mind. Until you establish a dialogue using symbols, the subconscious mind will not allow you to reach that deeper source of information.

Today, many people are attracted to ancient deities from around the world. This attraction may be to the deities of their ancestors, or it may come from a past life to which they still have strong ties.

Renewing a relationship with the powers represented by these old goddesses and gods by placing representations of them on altars may help these people improve their lives.

If you have no attraction to ancient deities, I you can choose to have representations of angels, archangels, and saints.

By using any of the following images and objects on your altars, you are strengthening the spiritual energies that collect about your sacred places. By intensifying the energies, you deepen your spiritual experience and hasten the creation of your desires.

## Sacred Animals

All around the world, various creatures have always represented certain deities and/or magickal qualities. Using statues, photos, or drawing of animals on your altar can help you to invoke a specific energy you wish to manifest in yourself or in your life. These animals can be actual creatures, or they can be what are known as fabulous beasts, such as the unicorn.

Following is a list of creatures, both physical and fabulous, whose magickal-spiritual qualities have been known and used by many cultures. Sometimes called shamanic or totem animals, their astral (nonphysical) equivalents frequently appear in meditations, shamanic journeys, and dreams.

**ADDER, SNAKE** Wisdom, cunning, defense, psychic energy, creative power, pure divine energy, beginning and ending, and understanding.

**BADGER** Tenacity and unyielding courage.

**BAT** Gaining direction in difficult circumstances; avoiding obstacles, barriers, and troublesome people. In China, the bat is a symbol of good fortune and happiness; in Europe, a companion creature of the goddess Hel.

**BEAR** Stamina, harmony, protecting the self and the family, dreams, intuition, transformation, and astral travel. The bear was sacred to the Greek goddesses Callisto and Artemis.

**BEE** Responsibility, cooperation, prosperity, and planning for the future. In the Indo-Aryan and Greek Orphic teachings, bees were thought of as souls. They were called the Little Servants of the Goddess by early matriarchies. Bee was also the title of Aphrodite's high priestess on Mount Eryx. The Greek goddess Demeter was sometimes called "the mother bee."

**BLACKBIRD** This bird denotes joy.

**BOAR** Cunning, intelligence, revenge, defense, knowledge of past lives, magick, protection of family, cooperation, prosperity, and health, death, and rebirth. The sow, in particular, represents magick, the Underworld, and deep knowledge of the Crone aspect of the Goddess. The sow was sacred to Astarte, Cerridwen, Demeter, Freyja, and the Buddhist aspect of the Goddess called Marici.

**BULL** The bull is a symbol of strength, potency, alertness, protection of the family, and knowing when to be aggressive. The cow represents gentleness and balance, but also fierce mother love and the life-giving and sustaining power of creation. In the beginning of human religious symbology, the bull was a lunar symbol of the Great Mother, with the horns emblematic of the crescent moon. Later, the bull became a symbol of sun gods such as Attis and Mithra, both associated with Cybele. The cow was associated with the Egyptian goddesses Hathor and Neith, and the Norse goddess Audhumla.

**BUTTERFLY** Reincarnation, beauty, love, transformation, joy, and freedom. To the ancient Greeks, the butterfly represented the soul. In Ireland, Cornwall, Mexico, and Siberia, white butterflies are still believed to be the spirits of the dead.

**CAT** Independence, discrimination, stealth, resourcefulness, healing, love, self-assurance, seeking hidden information, seeing spirits, and receiving

protection when faced with a confrontational situation. In ancient Egypt, the cat was considered to be a lunar creature and was sacred to Bast and Isis. In other cultures, it was sacred to Artemis, Diana, and Freyja.

**COBRA** To the ancient Egyptians, the cobra symbolized spiritual and divine wisdom and protection. The Hindus saw the cobra as a representation of the Kundalini force that rose through the seven chakras of the astral body.

**COCK** Self-confidence.

**COYOTE** Cunning, shapeshifting, stealth, opportunity, creativity, and new life.

**CRANE** From China to the Mediterranean, the crane represented justice, longevity, dignity, wisdom, discipline, vigilance, and reaching deeper mysteries and truths.

**CROCODILE** To ancient Egyptians, this creature represented mindless fury and evil. However, they also said the crocodile could provide knowledge.

**CROW** Trickery, boldness, skill, cunning, alertness, prophecy, and shape-shifting. A companion of the Celtic goddess Morrigan, the crow symbolized the creative power and spiritual strength found through the Crone aspect of the Goddess. The raven is similar.

**DEER, HIND, DOE** A messenger from the Otherworld, the appearance of the deer traditionally signaled a guide for adventures of mystical value. This creature also represented contact with spirit guides and the gods; abundance, dreams, intuition, and psychic powers.

**DOG** Devotion, companionship, loyalty, willingness to follow through, alertness, and discovering hidden knowledge and the truth. Sacred to Underworld goddesses, dogs also represented our own subconscious judgment. Myth says that the Celtic god Nodens, a healer, could shapeshift into a dog. The Norse god Odin rode on his Wild Hunt with a pack of hounds, carrying out the wishes of the goddess Hel.

**DOLPHIN** Intelligence, communication, friendships, eloquence, freedom, speed, prudence, change, balance, and harmony. Sacred to the Greek goddess Themis, this creature also symbolized active seedforms within the sea-womb of creation.

**DOVE** Often the symbol of a spiritual messenger between worlds, in the past this bird also represented peace and love, a meaning it still holds today. It was sacred to Aphrodite, Astarte, and Venus.

**DRAGON** This fabulous creature is a universal symbolic figure found in most cultures around the world, and has several, sometimes contradictory, meanings. The dragon represents cunning, knowledge, riches, protection, the ability to rise above and conquer obstacles, and instruction in spiritual matters.

**DRAGONFLY** Dreams, breaking down illusions, mystic messages of enlightenment, and seeing the truth in any situation.

**EAGLE** Wisdom, long life, taking advantage of opportunities, keen insight, strength, courage, seeing the overall pattern of life, connecting with powerful spiritual beings, and the ability to reach spiritual heights.

**ELEPHANT** A sacred creature to the Hindus, the elephant represents the power of the libido, removal of obstacles and barriers, confidence, patience, tackling a new situation, strength, wisdom, and eternity.

**FALCON** Astral travel and healing.

**FISH** To many Mediterranean and Asian cultures, fish in general symbolized sexuality and fertility. They also represent the subconscious mind and divination.

**FOX** The Greek god Dionysus was said to shapeshift into a fox on occasion; his Lydian priestesses wore fox skins and were called Bassarids. The fox denotes intelligence, cunning, wisdom, remaining unobserved, and avoiding trouble.

**FROG** Moving quickly, keeping a low profile, fertility, a new cycle of life, and initiation and transformation. The Egyptian frog goddess Hekat was connected with birth.

**GOOSE** New beginnings, inspiration, happiness in general, happy marriage, children, creativeness, and spiritual guidance in one's destiny.

**HARE** Transformation, receiving hidden teachings and intuitive messages, quick thinking, divination, fertility, swiftness, and avoiding traps or dangerous situations. Hares and rabbits were sacred to lunar goddesses.

**HAWK** Keen insight into situations, being observant, omens and dreams, and recalling past lives. In Egypt, the hawk was thought to represent the soul. Sacred to the god Horus, the hawk symbolized the inner vehicle for transformation. The hawk was also an animal of Apollo.

**HERON** Dignity, watching for opportunities, patience, and the generation of life.

**HIPPOPOTAMUS** Birth of new ideas, pregnancy, life, and strength. The Egyptian hippopotamus goddess Ta-Urt also represented righteous fury.

**HORSE** Associated in several cultures with death and the Underworld, the horse was frequently sacred to ocean deities. It was considered to be a vehicle for journeying to the Underworld, where one could contact spirits of the dead. It also symbolized freedom, friendships, stamina, faithfulness, and a journey.

**IBIS** A bird of the Egyptian god Thoth, the ibis was symbolic of magick, spells, writing, and recordkeeping.

**LEOPARD, PANTHER** Swiftness, cunning, strength, aggressiveness, and perseverance. These animals were sacred to the Greek god Dionysus.

**LION, LIONESS** The male lion represents relaxation, strengthening family ties, power, majesty, courage, energy, releasing tension and stress. The lioness symbolizes strong, protective mother love, the ability to care for one's self and family, and the strength to defeat aggressors. The lioness was sacred to such goddesses as Hathor, Sekhmet, and Cybele, while the lion belongs to such male deities as Apollo, Chrysocomes, the Arabic Shams-On, and Mithra.

**LIZARD** Escape from danger, dreams, mental creations, keeping a low profile, and asking for guidance in difficult situations.

**MONKEY** Ingenuity when dealing with problems.

**MOUSE** Being inconspicuous.

**OCTOPUS** Symbolizes the unfolding of the creative destructive process.

**OTTER** Magick, friendship, joy of life, finding inner treasures or talents, gaining wisdom, and recovering from a crisis.

**OWL** To the ancient Egyptians, the owl symbolized death, night, and cold. However, to the Greeks, it represented wisdom, the moon, lunar mysteries, and initiations. This bird also symbolizes alertness, wisdom, magick, keen insight into obscure events, unmasking deceivers, dreams, shapeshifting, clairvoyance, and a messenger of hidden secrets. The owl was sacred to such goddesses as the Eye Goddess of the Mediterranean, Athena, Lilith, Minerva, Blodeuwedd, Anath, and Mari.

**PEACOCK** Dignity, self-confidence, watchfulness, and divine justice. It was sacred to the goddesses Hera and Sarasvati.

**PHOENIX** Renewal, rebirth, and spiritual growth.

**RAM** Keeping your balance in upsetting situations, fertility, and new beginnings.

**RAT** Slyness and being able to move inconspicuously.

**RAVEN** This bird has long been considered a messenger from the spirit world and a guide to oracles and teachers of magick. Sacred to Celtic goddesses such as Rhiannon and Morrigan, the raven represents great magick, divination, eloquence, spiritual wisdom, prophecy, a change in consciousness, intelligence, and communicating with the Otherworld.

**SALMON** Great magick, journeys, endurance, and spiritual wisdom.

**SCARAB BEETLE** Vitality, new life, and learning about past lives.

**SEAL** Guidance when facing a separation or divorce, protection from gossip.

**SNAIL** This creature, with its spiral-shaped shell, represents the action of the primordial spiral of energy upon matter.

**SPHINX** Initiation and the end of a cycle.

**SPIDER** Creativity, new life, beginning a new project, and becoming pregnant. As a weaver, the spider symbolizes the spiraling energy of primordial matter and the Divine Center in the web of illusion.

**SQUIRREL** Harmony with life, patience, endurance, changing with the times, preparing for the future, and moving to a higher level of consciousness.

**STAG** This horned creature represents the animal passions within each human.

**STORK** Sacred to the goddess Juno, the stork represents a messenger of new ideas and birth.

**SWAN** Dream interpretation, mystical knowledge, developing intuitive abilities, dignity, and following instincts. Sacred to such goddesses as Aphrodite, Venus, Sarasvati, and the Norse Valkyries, the swan also symbolizes a messenger from the Goddess and the satisfaction of a desire.

**TIGER** Power, energy, facing an unpleasant situation and doing something about it.

**TURTLE, TORTOISE** Keeping alert for danger; patience, perseverance, long life. In the Far East, the turtle symbolized the cosmos and seeds of unformed matter that would subsequently manifest.

**VULTURE** Cycle of death and rebirth, spiritual counsel, destruction followed by rebirth, and prophecy. Sacred to the Egyptian goddesses Nekhbet and Mut.

**WHALE** Music, long life, family, friends, developing psychic and telepathic abilities, intuition and rebirth, and embracing the opposites of existence.

**WOLF** This animal represents cunning, intelligence, independence, avoiding trouble, and escaping pursuers, the ability to pass by danger invisibly, outwitting those who wish you harm, strength to fight when necessary, wisdom, dreams, intuition, transformation, strong protection, strength, and spiritual guidance. To the Egyptians and Romans, the wolf represented valor; the wolf-god Wepwawet was a companion of Isis and Osiris. Among the Norse, it symbolized the destructive powers of chaos; Odin had two great wolves by his side at all times. The wolf was sacred to the Roman Lupa or Feronia and was a symbolic animal of the Vestal Virgins.

## Ritual Objects

Throughout human history, symbols and physical objects have been used in ritual and art to represent spiritual ideas. Many of these physical and artistic metaphors are still being used in modern religions and are powerful symbols for spiritual development. They often appear spontaneously in dreams and visions.

Any object becomes sacred when it is used consciously for the proper reasons on the altar. The following list suggests items you might wish to use. However, any object that has meaning for you is just as appropriate.

**ANKH** A life symbol of a cross with a loop on top, the ankh was used by the ancient Egyptians to represent eternal life and resurrection. The crook or crozier, also known as the Shepherd's Cross, is a similar symbol. The

Egyptian god Osiris, in his role as Shepherd of Souls, carried a crook, as did the Greek Hermes. Use it to represent divine guidance and spiritual seeking.

**ARROWS** This emblem signifies divine intervention of both healing and killing power. To the Balkans god Perun, the arrow denoted lightning, long a symbol of illumination. A symbol of the god Apollo, the arrow also represents supreme power and the sun's fertile rays. Mars, Tyr, and Mithra were also associated with the arrow. Use the arrow to symbolize the direct path you plan to take.

**BASKET** A sign of fertility, passion, and birth, a basket of ivy in ancient Greece symbolized the Bacchanalian mysteries of Dionysus. In ancient Egyptian hieroglyphs, it represented the wholeness of divinity. Ceremonies to the Egyptian goddess Isis and the Greek Artemis featured sacred baskets. Place a basket on your altar to symbolize gathering what you need in life.

**BOWL** A symbol of the universal womb, the bowl represents both nurturing and giving. Use it to hold special stones or paper requests.

**BOX** With a lid, this is a female symbol connected with the subconscious mind and the unknown. A box without a lid represents life or gifts coming to you; it represents the universal womb. As with the basket and bowl, you can place in the box requests written on pieces of paper or jewelry that you wish to empower.

**BRIDGE** Traditionally, the bridge is a link between heaven and earth, or between the subconscious and conscious minds. Bifrost was the astral bridge that spanned the heavens between Asgard and Midgard in Norse myth, while for the Israelites the bridge symbolized the Covenant between God and His people. An image of a bridge can represent the bridging of differences, making a transition from one cycle of life to another, or moving to a higher plane of consciousness.

**BRIDLE** This is a symbol of control over the physical body and the emotional things that would motivate a person to react without clear thinking.

**CADUCEUS** Most people are familiar with the wand with two entwined serpents as the emblem of the Greek god Hermes and healing. However, this emblem existed long before the Greeks used it. The Sumerian goddess

Inanna is shown holding the caduceus as she stands under the Tree of Life. The double-headed snake was one of the emblems of Ningishzide, a healer god who was one of Ishtar's lovers. The caduceus is also found on stone tablets in India, in paintings by Native Americans, and in Aztec art. To the Romans, it was a symbol of moral equilibrium, while to Buddhists it represents the axis of the world with the kundalini of the chakras entwined about it.

**CANDLES** Lighted candles symbolize personal spiritual enlightenment. When Different colors have different meanings.

**CAULDRON** Long a holy object, the cauldron represents the belly-vessel of rebirth and transformation. It was associated with many goddesses, one of whom was the Celtic Cerridwen. Use a small cauldron to symbolize the churning, primordial matter from which you can draw energy to manifest your desires.

**CHALICE, CUP** Similar to the cauldron, the chalice has several meanings. Its primary meaning is rebirth and illumination. However, a filled chalice represents the bounty of life coming to you from a higher power, while an empty chalice is the receptacle for offerings. To rid yourself of negative emotions and feelings, gently blow into an empty cup, mentally emptying yourself of your problems. Then, turn the cup upside down on the altar. This symbolizes your turning your problems over to a higher power to be solved and transformed.

**CHILD** The image of a child symbolizes the future with its potential as yet unrealized, the deeply hidden treasure in the mystic center of each human, or the beginning of a new cycle.

**CIRCLE** An ancient symbol, the circle represents the return from multiples to unity, from time to timelessness, from body-obsessed consciousness to the spiritually centered subconscious. Jung calls the circle the ultimate state of Oneness, for it has no beginning and no end. Engravings of circles and cups can be seen in Paleolithic caves and Neolithic graves. The Gnostics used a drawing of a snake with its tail in its mouth to represent the circle; this symbol was called the ouroboros and it represented the cycles of time, life, the universe, death, and rebirth. The Native Americans made and still make circular medicine wheels. Permanent circles often marked holy places and sacred sites, such as Stonehenge and the Chinese Temple of Heaven. To several ancient cultures, the black circle represented the sun god during his nightly passage through the Underworld. Sometimes, instead of the sun god, it symbolized his dark twin brother, a secret, very wise god who held knowledge about all worlds. Modern Wiccans and magicians draw a circle about their ritual area to symbolize protection from negative astral forces and to represent moving beyond the material world's vibrations.

**CLOVER OR TREFOIL** Long before Christianity arose, the clover, or any three-leafed plant, was an emblem of the Triple Goddess; among Christians, it became the symbol of the Trinity. All trinity symbols date back to the time of the Goddess religions when they represented the Maiden, Mother, and Crone aspects of the Goddess. As far back as the civilization in the Indus Valley (c. 2500- 1700 BCE), the trefoil emblem signified a triple deity.

**COBWEB** Associated with the Fate goddesses and weaving, the cobweb is the spiral shape of the creative matrix that leads inward to the center where matter is destroyed before being reformed. Minerva, Athena, and Spider Woman are associated with spiders and cobwebs.

**COLUMN, TREE, LADDER, OBELISK** Symbolic of the connection between heaven and earth, or gods and mortals, this emblem has been pictured as a ladder, column, World Tree, sacred mountain, obelisk of the sun god, or tent pole of the shamans. It is much the same symbol as the bridge. When in pairs, the columns signify the balancing of opposing forces.

**CORNUCOPIA** This horn of plenty, usually filled with fruits and vegetables, symbolizes strength, abundance, and prosperity.

**CRESCENT** The crescent is a lunar and Goddess symbol. It represents the world of changing forms that goes through a cycle to repeat itself endlessly.

**CROSS** Now a Christian symbol, the cross is actually a very ancient symbol, meaning much the same as the column. However, the crosspiece of the emblem signifies the balance of the four elements. The cross was associated with the Phoenician goddess Astarte, the Greek deities Artemis and Aphrodite, and the Aztec goddess of rain.

**CROWN** In cultures as far apart as India and northern Europe, the crown symbolized the sacred marriage between the Goddess and Her consort. This emblems signifies light, achievement, success, and spiritual enlightenment.

**CUBE** The three-dimensional equivalent of the square, this symbol represents the material world of the four elements. It is also associated with stability. A box with a lid can be a cube into which you place your requests on slips of paper.

**CURL, LOOP, ROPE** As with the knot, this emblem means binding and unbinding, especially in a magickal or spiritual sense.

**CURTAIN, VEIL** The veil represents the ethereal door between the worlds of matter and spirit. Seven veils were associated with the goddesses Ishtar and Isis.

**DICE** These represent gambling with the Fates; taking chances.

**DISK** A sun emblem, the disk symbolizes matter in a state of transformation. Associated with the sun, the disk also signifies celestial perfection.

**DOOR, GATE, PORTAL** Any door signifies the entrance to the path leading to spirit, an initiation, or the opening of a new talent or way of life. In addition, the door represents the ability to pass from the earth to the astral plane, from one cycle of life to another, or to another level of spiritual knowledge. Similar to circles, doors also symbolize a separation of the physical and the sacred, signaling to the subconscious mind that a mindset transition must be made. The two-faced Roman god Janus, deity of the past and the future, ruled over doorways of all kinds. Altars were frequently placed near doors in ancient Greece, Rome, and Mexico.

**DRUM** This instrument symbolizes divine ecstasy in ritual. In Africa, the drum is associated with the heart, while other cultures that practice any form of shamanism believe it is a mediator between earth and heaven.

**EAR OF CORN** Associated with many harvest deities, including Ceres and Demeter, an ear of corn represents the disintegration of life followed by rebirth. It also symbolizes the germination and growth of ideas. Maize or grains or corn represent prosperity and fertility.

**EGG** Eggs dyed red were an important part of early Goddess worship and ritual, especially in spring. In ancient Egypt, the hieroglyph of an egg represented the potential seed of rebirth. Several creation myths tell the story of the World Egg. This symbol signifies immortality and the potential for life renewal.

**EYE** Thousands of statues of the Eye Goddess have been excavated from third-millennium Sumer, where this aspect of the Goddess was very sacred. In Egypt, the eye was associated primarily with the god Horus. The eye is associated with intelligence, spiritual light, intuition, and truth that cannot be hidden. It also represents judgment by the Goddess.

**FAN** Femininity, intuition, and change. The fan is an emblem of the Chinese deity Chung-Li Chuan, one of the Eight Chinese immortals.

**FEATHER, PLUME** In Egypt, the feather of truth was associated with the goddess Maat. It represents faith, contemplation, and reincarnating souls. Many goddesses,

including Juno, were associated with feathers, which represent change.

**FLOWER** Flowers are usually connected with spring and rebirth or renewal. For a more complete explanation of flowers, read the Flowers chart on this page.

**FOUNTAIN** The main portion of the fountain is associated in a minor way with the World Tree, while the flowing water represents the life force within all things. The fountain symbolizes blessings, wisdom, purification, renewal, and comfort arising from the Divine Center.

**GEODE** A womb symbol.

**GLOBE, SPHERE** Representing the world soul and the human soul, the globe or sphere symbolizes wholeness. If it is depicted with wings, it represents spiritual evolution.

**GOBLET** The same as the chalice and cauldron.

**GRAIN, WHEAT, CORN** This emblem represents life and the sustaining of it, and the harvest.

**GRAPES** Associated with such gods as Dionysus, grapes represent fertility and sacrifice.

**HAND** Handprints are among the first symbols found in ancient, sacred Paleolithic caves. There, red marks of individual hands are found among wavy lines for water and crescent-shaped horns of fertility. In the shrines of matriarchal Catal Huyuk in seventh-millennium Anatolia, handprints, along with butterflies, bees, and the heads of bulls, decorate the walls. In Catal Huyuk, the hand probably represented the hand of the Goddess and action or manifestation, while in ancient Egypt, when combined with an eye, it signified clairvoyant action. In present Islamic cultures, the hand is still sacred and symbolizes protection, power, and strength.

**HARP** Similar to the World Tree or mystic ladder, the harp is another symbol of the bridge between heaven and earth.

**HEART** The ancient Egyptians believed that thoughts and morals arose from the heart, the center of physical life and a symbol of eternity. Thus, this symbol represents moral judgment, and pure, true love.

**HEXAGRAM OR SIX-POINTED STAR** The six-pointed star is comprised of two overlapping triangles oriented in opposite directions, and is found around the world. It is known as the Seal of Solomon, David's Shield, or the Star of David (in Judaism). The hexagram represents the combination of male and female.

**HONEY** To the Greek Orphists, honey was a symbol of wisdom. In India, it symbolizes the higher self.

**HORNS** Originally a fertility and lunar symbol, to early cultures horns also represented strength, power, and prosperity. The Egyptian hieroglyph of the horn signified elevation, prestige, and glory. The word horned may be derived form the Assyro-Babylonian garnu of the Phoenician words geren, gamuim, or kerenos. The horned Apollo Karnaios resembles the horned Celtic god Cernunnos.

**HORSESHOE** Originally a symbol of the Goddess, the horseshoe represents the ending of one cycle and the beginning of another.

**HOURGLASS** This emblem symbolizes the cycle and connection between the upper (spiritual) and lower (physical) worlds, creation and destruction.

**JAR, URN** Long a sacred object in many cultures, a pot or jar represents the universal womb of the Goddess and the Oneness that proceeds from the Great Mother. It symbolizes the potential for transforming anything placed inside it. In China, the jar represents good luck. Isis was frequently portrayed with a jar about her neck, just as the Hindu goddess Kali was shown with pots and jars. Many sacred ceremonies involved the use of water jars to signify the presence of the deities. These ceremonies included the Osirian Mysteries of Egypt, the Babylonian rites of the god Nabu, the Cabirian Mysteries for Demeter and Cabirius, and the Greek festival of Anthesteria for Dionysus.

**KEYS** The symbol is associated with many deities from a variety of cultures. Hecate and Persephone held the keys to the Underworld and the universe. Athena was said to control the key to the city of Athens. The Babylonian god Marduk is said to have made the keys to heaven and hell that only Ishtar could use. In Rome, women in labor were given keys to hold for an easy childbirth. The Egyptian god Serapis was believed to have the keys to both the earth and the sea. Ancient spiritual mysteries speak of keys as the symbol of knowledge, a task to be performed, or a successful question or spiritual journey. Keys are still used as a symbol of warding off evil spirits, and represent the means of solving a mystery or performing a task. They are also symbols of locking and unlocking, or binding and loosening.

**KNIFE** While the sword symbolizes spiritual heights, the knife represents vengeance, death, and sacrifice; it also alludes to the means to end a cycle.

**KNOT** The knot has two meanings: unity, stopping progress, or binding up energies when it is tied, but also releasing energy when untied. It is closely associated with weaving and the woven web of life. This symbol, with its weaving connotations, was connected with the Greek Fate goddesses and the Norse Norns. In ancient Egypt, Isis was said to loosen or bind the knot of life, while Hathor wore a menat, the knotted headband or necklace. All the Egyptian holy mysteries were called "she-knots." The knot can be found in the Egyptian circle of eternity, the loop of the ankh, and the cartouche that circles the name of a pharaoh. Priestesses of the Goddess in Crete wore a knot of hair at the back of their heads and hung a knot of cloth at the entrance to the shrines. In Rome, it was forbidden for anyone to wear anything knotted or tied within the precinct of Juno, who was the goddess of childbirth; knots were thought to cause a difficult birth. Muslims will not wear knots when they take their pilgrimage to Mecca. According to rabbinical law, Jews are not to tie knots on the Sabbath. One of the Chinese emblems of good luck is the Buddhist "endless knot" of longevity. Among the Celts, the knot was a protective device to trap negative or evil energies.

Tie knots in strings or yarn to bind up negative energy. Or use intricate drawings of knotwork to release energy when it is needed.

**LABYRINTH** The labyrinth takes its name from the ancient Minoan labrys, or double ax. However, the idea and use of the labyrinth in drawings goes back much further than Crete. Such designs are found on the walls of Paleolithic caves, where the ritual participants had to crawl through narrow openings and traverse narrow passageways to reach the sacred center of the cave itself. This symbol represents the spiritual path leading back to the Divine Center, regeneration through the Goddess by the process of initiative rebirth. Focus on a drawing of a labyrinth while tracing the path with your finger. This will draw you toward the spiritual center of your being.

**LAMP** This emblem symbolizes spiritual intelligence and enlightenment. The Hermit of the tarot cards is shown holding a lamp or lantern, denoting his offering of guidance and higher instruction. Deities associated with the lamp were Juno Lucina and Diana Lucifera.

**LEAF** T O the Chinese, the leaf means happiness.

**MASK** In ancient times, the mask was worn during Mystery rituals to signify the spiritual metamorphosis conferred by the rite itself. This emblem represents secrecy, hidden meanings, and shapeshifting.

**MIRROR** A Goddess and moon symbol whose meanings include revealing the truth, intuition, and the psychic realm, and the imagination. Mirrors were also known as soul-catchers or soul-carriers; Celtic women were buried with their mirrors that they believed carried their souls.

**MOON** Originally a symbol of many goddesses and a few gods, the moon later came to symbolize the rhythm of life and the universe, the passage of time, and the power of rebirth. The moon represents creation, ripeness, cycles of life, spiritual disciplines, and initiations.

**NECKLACE** At one time a sexual symbol of the completeness of the Goddess, the threaded, beaded necklace later came to mean the unity of diversity, or the continuity of the past lives of a human. The goddesses Freyja and Ishtar wore special necklaces.

**NEST** This symbol represents the foundation or beginning of a life, event, or path.

**OAR** This mundane object represents action, controlling the direction life is taking, and stability within an unstable situation.

**OBELISK** Primarily a symbol of ancient Egypt, the obelisk was an emblem of the sun god and considered to be a solidified ray of the sun. Physically, it was a slender, four-sided, tapering column that could be hundreds of feet high. Obelisks frequently stood beside the doors of temples. The door to the temple of the goddess Astarte at Byblos was flanked by a pair of obelisks.

**PALACE, CASTLE** This emblem represents the sacred place

within, or the Divine Center.

**PAPYRI, BOOK** Whether a rolled scroll or a bound book, the symbol means knowledge and an unfolding of the Akashic Records. These Records are a spiritual compilation of all the lives of every person.

**PEACH** To the Asians, the peach symbolizes immortality.

**PEARL** Considered one of the eight Chinese emblems, the pearl signifies the sacred center. To Muslims, it represents heaven or paradise.

**PENTACLE, PENTAGRAM** A pentacle is a five-pointed star, once the symbol of all things feminine and the great Earth Mother. In Egyptian hieroglyphs, it means to "rise up" or "cause to arise," and it was associated with both Isis and Nephthys. The pentacle was also a symbol of the Babylonian Ishtar and the Celtic Morrigan. To the Gnostics, it represented the sacred number five, while for Pythagoreans it meant harmony of the body and mind. The five-pointed star was also associated with the Virgin Mary in her aspect of Stella Maris (Star of the Sea). This symbol represents the repulsion of evil, or protection.

**PINECONE** A product of the pine tree, which symbolizes immortality, the cone represents psychic oneness. It was one of the symbols of both Astarte in ancient Byblos and the sacrificed savior Attis. The sacred wand of Dionysus, called the thyrsus, was tipped with a pinecone, as was that of the Roman Bacchus.

**PLAIT, BRAID** Long associated with rope and knots, the braid represents the intertwining of relationships or creative matter.

**POMEGRANATE** The Greek Underworld goddess Persephone was linked with the pomegranate, thus giving it the meaning of the dead lying in sleep before rebirth. Deities associated with this fruit were Persephone, Dionysus, Adonis, Attis, and the Crone aspect of the Goddess.

**PUMPKIN** An emblem of Li Tieh-Kuai, one of the Chinese Immortals, the pumpkin represents a link between two worlds. It can also mean an upheaval in the usual order.

**PYRAMID** Similar in meaning to the triangle, the pyramid is actually a hollow mountain. It symbolizes rebirth, regeneration, and creation.

**RAINBOW** Similar to the bridge, ladder, and obelisk, the rainbow represents the connection between earth and the sky, or the mundane world and the sacred. The Greek goddess Iris carried messages from the gods to humans on this celestial bridge. In the middle East, the rainbow symbolized the veils of Ishtar and, in the Far East, the illusive veils of Maya. Among the Pueblo and Navajo Indians, the rainbow was known as the road of the spirits and gods.

**RING** Similar to the circle, the ring represents continuity and wholeness. When associated with the Fates, it symbolizes the eternally repeated cycle of time.

**SCALES** First seen in Chaldean carvings, the scales symbolize justice, cause and effect, the divine assessment of a life. Deities associated with this emblem were Maat and Astraea.

**SCEPTER** Related to the magick wand, the thunderbolt, the phallus, and Thor's hammer, the scepter represents fertility, purification, and the ability and willpower to make changes.

**SCISSORS** A symbol of both life and death, scissors were associated with the Fates and other deities who ruled over the length of life.

**SCYTHE** Connected with the god Saturn and with the moon, the scythe represents reaping the harvest, or the harvest when the life-path is finished.

**SHEAF, BUNDLE** Related to knots, the sheaf symbolizes unification and strength, but also limitation because of the binding.

**SHELL** To Chinese Buddhists, the shell is one of the eight emblems of good luck. It is related to the moon, the sea, and all sea deities. The spiral form of the shell represents the life force moving toward the sacred center.

**SHIELD** Protection, identity.

**SHIP** The journey through physical life, or the inner, spiritual journey.

**SIEVE** Sorting out, purifying, discarding the useless.

**SPIRAL** Connected with both the snake and the labyrinth, the spiral is an ancient sacred symbol. Spirals appear on Paleolithic sacred sites and objects, and represent the awesome powers of death and rebirth, a process Pagans and Zirceans believe is held only by the Goddess. The spiral signifies the unfolding of potent, creative energy.

**SQUARE** Symbolic of the four elements, the square represents order and direction. It is considered to be of feminine nature with strong connections to the earth. Egyptian hieroglyphs used the square to mean achievement. Carl Jung believed this symbol signified the unachieved state of inner unity. The square represents definition, stability, and firmness.

**STAFF** Support, authority.

**STAR** To many cultures, the star signified the dead; in Judaism it is believed that each star has a guardian angel. The Aztecs said that stars were the regenerated spirits of fallen or sacrificed warriors. The star symbolizes spirit shining in the darkness of the labyrinth and a beacon to guide the pilgrim on the journey through the subconscious.

**SWASTIKA** Although not likely to appeal to most people today, this symbol had a long history of deep, spiritual meaning before it was perverted by the Nazis. The name actually comes from the Sanskrit words su, "good," and asti, "being." Connected with both the sun and the moon, it signifies movement and regenerative power.

**SWORD** Strength, defense.

**THUNDERBOLTS** Celestial fire, illumination, chance, destiny, associated with Zeus, Jupiter, Shiva, Pyerun, and Thor.

**TOWER** Rising above the physical, ascent of the spirit.

**TRIANGLE** This was an early symbol of the feminine principle. In Paleolithic times, skulls were often buried under triangular rocks, representing the Goddess's power of rebirth. For the Pythagoreans, the Greek letter delta (a triangle) symbolized cosmic birth. The triangle was associated with the Hindu goddess Durga, the Celtic Triple Goddess, the Greek Moerae, the Nordic Norns, and the triple Roman Fortunae. The triangle symbolizes body, mind, and spirit, and therefore represents the Triple Goddess.

**TRUMPET** Fame and glory; warning; elements of Fire and Air.

**VASE** An ancient symbol of repose, life, and fertility, vases with breasts have been dated back to the sixth millennium BCE. During rituals, these breast-vases were filled with a liquid that was sprinkled through the nipples onto the offering and worshippers. The Chinese goddess Kuan Yin often holds a vase in one hand.

**WATER** Primal matter, universal possibilities.

**WHEEL** The wheel differs from the circle in that it has spokes that divide it. To the Romans, the wheel was an emblem of the goddess Fortuna, who ruled the fate or changing fortunes of humans. The wheel of the Hindu goddess Kali is the wheel of karma. The Buddhists call the wheel the Holy Wheel of Life, while the Celts used an eight-spoked wheel to represent their sacred year with its eight sacred festivals. Today, the wheel is commonly seen as one of the Major Arcana cards in tarot decks, where it represents the changing cycles of fortune. Frequently, the wheel is a solar symbol and connected with sun gods. It signifies spiritual advancement or regression, and the progression of karma, which is payment of good and evil done in a life.

**WINGS** In many ancient carvings and drawings, wings denoted the divine and were added to figures of deities or sacred objects. Wings represent ideas, thoughts, spirituality, imagination, mobility, and enlightenment.

**YIN/YANG SYMBOL** This Asian symbol is a circle divided into half-white and half-black by a curving S. It represents perfect balance.

# Chapter 9: The Sacred Circle and Raising Power

## Creating the Perfect Environment for Working Magic

Sacred space and a cast, magick circle are two entirely different principles that meet during ritual and magick to become one. You don't have to cast a circle in sacred space; likewise, you don't need physical sacred space to cast a circle. Notice the words I use here: don't have to and don't need. Calling on the Gods and Goddesses will work regardless of where you are or in what circumstances you find yourself. It will work as long as the intention is there – even if you don't have a single candle or stick of incense so don't get too caught up in getting everything 100% correct.

In essence, all life and all places are sacred. To defile the air we breathe and the ground upon which we walk is to defile ourselves and our planet. Our planet is a sacred space in the Universe, as are the other planets and heavenly bodies. Sacred space can be a natural reservoir of energy, such as a stream, a mountain, a field, and so on.

That said, just because you don't need to cast a circle, it doesn't mean you shouldn't do so. Casting a circle can help to focus and direct your energies and can help you to more effectively draw the power that you need to make use of them.

# Chapter 10: Spell Casting

## How to Cast Successful Spells

Once you have become comfortable in casting circles and in casting spells, you will want to create your own spells as well.

Learning more about how to create spells that are powerful is an important part of your progress as a Wiccan. A spell designed by you is more powerful to you because of the fact that you designed it.

In Wicca, sympathetic magic plays a big role and we tend to try and work with "correspondences". This basically means matching the right spell with the correct day of the week, lunar phase, particular symbols. colors and deities in order to achieve maximum benefit.

The various correspondences are too many to go into here in great detail but you should do further research into them.

As a basic starting point, spells that are intended to bring something towards you, such as prosperity spells, are best performed when the moon is waxing (getting bigger) and spells that are aimed at getting rid of something (like illness) are best performed when the moon is waning (getting smaller).

All a spell is a spoken or written formula that, in an act of magic , is intended to cause or influence a course of events. Methods of spell-casting vary according to culture, but all spell work is based on ritual.

Spells are closely related to prayer, which is a ritual consisting of a petition to a deity or deities for a desired outcome, and which involves visualization of the goal and a statement of desire for the goal.

# Chapter 11: Writing Your Own Spells

## Create Your Own Spells for Any Occasion

Writing your own spells is pretty simple – a spell is a statement of intent more than anything else and can be as simple or complex as you want.

Start writing down what you want the spell to achieve and then phrase it in a simple manner so that it can be easily chanted. There is no need for it to be a wonderful piece of prose or poetry – it need not even rhyme. Simply make sure that the words come from the heart and be very specific about what it is that you want to achieve and you will find that the spell is successful.

As mentioned previously, all spells should end off with the phrase, "And harm none, so mote it be" so that no harm is done to anyone during the spell casting.

Once you have determined what the best terms for the spell are, look into choosing the most auspicious day for casting the spell, a deity to ask for assistance with the spell, any talismans, herbs, candles, etc. that can assist with the performance of the spell and whether the spell should be cast on a waxing or waning moon.

Once you have determined what is needed, gather everything together and get it ready for use on the appropriate day.

## Use Oils for Better Results

Candles are frequently rubbed with scented oil from wick to end (to attract something) or from end to wick (to repel something). As you do this, concentrate on the purpose you have in mind.

Candles can be used with only the oil, or oil and herbs.

If called for, roll the oiled candle in the appropriate crushed herbs, still thinking of

your goal.

Planetary oils are used when you desire to strengthen certain planetary energies in your life or in more advanced magickal spells.

## Use Incense as Well

It really does not matter if you use incense in powered form, cones, or sticks. You are using incense to set a particular magickal atmosphere. Choose scents suited to your purpose or substitute the all-purpose scents of lotus, frankincense, or frankincense and myrrh combined in either stick or cone form. You can even make your own incense for optimal results.

## Crystals and Stones

When using stones to amplify your spell work, there are two ways to choose them. You may use the general description by color to choose the stones you need, or you may use the more specific list by magical description.

Stones do not need to be faceted, fancy, or expensive to work. Stones found in a natural state or tumbled until smooth can be just as effective as expensive ones.

There are certain stones that can be used with any candle burning. Clear quartz crystal is so powerful and all embracing that you can substitute it for other stones or add it to groupings of other stones to amplify their energy. Fluorite also amplifies the energies of other stones, regardless of its color.

Carnelian will speed up the manifestation of your desire. Lodestone will help in any ritual where you are attempting to attract something into your life. The little-used spectrolite can manifest results in any situation that may require a "miracle" to see results.

It is important to cleanse your stones carefully before use. Cleansing can be done by washing the stones, placing them in salt or placing them in the earth. Read up a little on the properties of the stone you want to use to ensure it will not be damaged by your form of cleansing – Calcite and opals, for example, do not do well in water and turquoise should not be exposed to salt.

Your crystals should ideally be charged before use – this can be done by leaving them on the windowsill for at least 24 hours so that they are exposed to the sun and the moon. You can then pass them through the smoke of frankincense or myrrh incense to positively charge them.

When choosing which stones to use, take careful note of any that seem to jump out at you – you will instinctively be drawn to stones with properties that you need so take special care to trust this instinct.

To further improve the strength of your spell, you can anoint the stones with your chosen oil and keep them on your person at all times. You can either wear them in the form of jewelry or simply place them in the pocket of your jacket or pants. Alternatively, make a bag containing the herbs and items from your spells and keep this on your person as a kind of talisman.

The primary consideration here though is to handle the stones often so that they can impart their energy to you and so that you are reminded of the visualization that you created during the spell.

# Chapter 12: Spells for Attracting Abundance

## A Few Quick Abundance Spells for You

### A Prosperity Spell to Draw Money to You

You will need one of each of:

Dollar bill

Quarter

Buckeye

Basil

Cedar

Marigold

Lodestone

Bayberry oil

Green bag

Red string

Anoint the quarter, Buckeye, and the lodestone with Bayberry oil. Place the quarter eagle side up on top of the eagle on the dollar. Place the Buckeye on the coin. Fold bill toward you so that the All-Seeing Eye is showing. Tie up with red string. Place in the green bag. Add the herbs. Anoint the bag and the herbs with Bayberry Oil.

Charge with the following invocation:

*"My life is filled with abundance and all my needs are met, and harm none, so be it."* Repeat three times.

Carry with you and re-charge at least once a month.

## To Attract Money

Straight or votive candles as follows: one green (material gain), one brown (attract money), and one gold (financial benefits).

Bergamot or cinnamon oil

Nutmeg

Cinnamon or honeysuckle incense

Agate and garnet stones

A Small nail.

This spell should be performed on a Sunday either when the moon is full or when it is waxing.

This spell is for those times when you need a quick injection of cash, it won't make you rich.

Light the altar candles and the incense.

Using the nail, inscribe the brown candle with three dollar signs representing money: $$$. Below this, carve in the amount you need.

Anoint the candles from the wick to the end.

Set the brown candle in the center of your altar with your astrological candle behind it. Set the gold candle on the left of the brown candle and the green candle on the right. Place the agate between the gold and brown, and the garnet between the brown and green.

Light the candles from left to right.

Say the chant five times.

Leave the candles to burn out completely.

Dispose of the wax afterward.

Chant "One, two, three, four, money knocking on my door. Five, six, seven, eight, a jingling purse is my fate and harm none, so be it."

## Gain Prosperity

A green (material gain) seven-day, glass-enclosed candle or a double-action green candle and four orange (attraction, sudden changes, success) straight or votive candles.

Bayberry or bergamot oil

Vervain.

Bayberry or jasmine incense

Bloodstone and malachite stones

A small nail.

This should be performed on a Thursday when the moon is full or waxing.

Repeat periodically for consistent results.

Light the altar candles and the incense.

Using a nail, carve a dollar sign into the green portion of the double-action candle or into the top of the glass-enclosed candle.

Inscribe a lightning bolt into each of the orange candles.

Anoint the double-action candle and the orange candles from the wick to the end, or just the top of the enclosed candle.

Set it in the center of your altar.

Arrange the orange candles around the central green candle.

Place the malachite on one side of the central candle, the bloodstone on the other.

Light the central green candle, then the orange ones.

Say the chant.

Leave the candles to burn out completely.

Dispose of the wax afterward.

If you wish, you may burn four new orange candles each day until the seven-day green candle is gone.

Chant "Worries gone, finances clear, security comes for one full year. I wrap myself in prosperity and harm none, so be it."

## Get Someone to Repay What is Owed to You

A 7 day green candle and four yellow (gentle persuasion) straight or votive candles.

Jasmine oil

Clove – dried buds or powder

Ginger, jasmine, or allspice incense

Hematite and tiger's eye tumbled stones

Perform this spell on a Saturday when the moon is full or waxing.

Before you take the decision to cast this spell, you need to be 100% sure that the person does owe you the money. If not, this spell will backfire and you will end up repaying your own debts. If you have a friend or family member who always borrows stuff without returning it, this spell can also compel them to give your items back.

Light the altar candles and the incense.

Inscribe the name of the person who owes you the debt on the seven-knob green candle. Anoint the candles from the wick to the end.

Set the green candle in the center of your altar.

Set the yellow candles around the green one, with the stones inside this circle.

Light the green candle first, then the others.

Say the chant seven times.

Leave the yellow candles to burn out completely.

Dispose of the wax afterward.

Burn only one knob of the green candle each night.

If you wish, you may burn new yellow candles each night until the seven-knob candle is gone.

Chant "What was given in trust shall be freely returned. What was mine shall be mine again and harm none, so be it."

## Increase Personal Power

Straight or votive candles in the following colors: one silver (victory, stability), one yellow (confidence, concentration), and one purple (success, wisdom).

Carnation oil

Red sandalwood or rue.

Carnation, frankincense, or pine incense

Agate, jasper, and black obsidian tumbled stones

This spell is best performed on a Thursday when the moon is full or waxing.

The intention behind this spell is to build your self-esteem so that you can be more assertive, not so that you can gain control over someone else.

Light the altar candles and the incense.

Anoint the candles from the wick to the end.

The candles are set out in a triangular pattern with the silver at the top, the yellow at the bottom right, and the purple at the bottom left.

Place the black obsidian near the silver candle, the jasper near the yellow, and the agate

near the purple.

Light the candles in the same order, beginning with the silver.

Say the chant.

Leave the candles to burn out completely.

Dispose of the wax afterward.

Chant "Power of the self, I seek. Strength to be bold, not weak. Courage to stand straight and tall, power to overcome all and harm none, so be it."

## A Spell to Help with Success or Promotion

This is best used when the moon is waxing and best conducted on a Wednesday. You will call on Mercury, messenger of the Gods to help with this spell.

You will need:

1 Yellow candle

1 Charcoal disc

Matches

A dish that is fire-proof

3 Sycamore Seeds

½ a teaspoon of Benzoin

½ teaspoon of Lavender Seeds

Set the candle alight while chanting,

*"Mercury, fast and swift,*

*bring to me my dearest wish."*

Place the charcoal disc in the dish and set it alight. When it starts glowing red, place the Benzoin onto it and say, *"Success to me, and harm none, let it be."*

Next you will sprinkle on the Lavender seeds while saying, *"May my wish be fruitful and harm none."*

Once that is done, pick up the Sycamore Seeds and meditate on the success or promotion that you wish to achieve. Visualize having already achieved it. Inhale deeply and, when you let the breath out, visualize that success being transferred over to the seeds.

Place the seeds onto the disc and both burn out naturally.

Before the next sunrise, and once the ashes are cool, bury them in the earth under a plant that is thriving.

## A Spell to Increase your Psychic Abilities

This spell should be done during a full moon or a waxing moon.

You will need:

1 white candle

4 purple or lilac candles

Jasmine Incense

A notebook used only for this purpose

Cast your circle as normal. Place the purple candle at each cardinal point. Light your incense and then set the white candle directly in front of where you will sit. Light each candle, starting at the top and working your way around. The white candle should be last. While lighting the candles, start to clear your mind.

Once the white candle has been lit, gaze directly into its flame and visualize the center of your forehead and your third eye - visualize the energy from the flame of the candle being absorbed into your third eye and chant, as you are visualizing:

*"Vision of what is meant to be,*

*psychic views of history,*

*The power to hear what others cannot*

*The power to know my psychic lot.*

*Psychic powers I call to me*

*To see the things I wish to see*

*To know the things I wish to know.*

*Open my spirit and my mind*

*Psychic bonds to me do tie,*

*Let my mind be no more bound*

*until the answers I seek are found.*

*Allow me visions when day is done,*

*as I cast this spell, let it be done.*

*And harm none so be it."*

Once this ritual is done, snuff out all the candles and close off the circle.

Place the notebook and a pen on your bedside table and write down anything you can remember of your dreams, no matter how crazy they seem. At first, they may be confusing but over time you will learn to interpret what you see and what patterns emerge.

## A Spell to Increase Knowledge

This should be done when the moon is waxing or when it is full.

You will need:

Something that can be used as a cauldron - a cooking pot will do in need

Matches

1 White candle

Sage

Verbena or Vervain

A Bay leaf

A ladle or long-handled spoon

water

Cast your circle as normal. Light your candle while chanting the following, *"Cerridwen, The Great White Sow, grant me a taste of your wisdom, if you so allow."*

Put the water into your cauldron and add the verbena/ vervain; the sage and the bay lead. Stir slowly as you say:

*"Ten long years; a year or even a day, is to me too much of a delay, I humbly ask to be granted my wish, it is gaining arcane wisdom that is my most fervent wish."*

Place your thumb into the mixture and then, as you suck it clean, say, *"May this spell open my mind, and let me learn the wisdom here combined, Give me the wisdom I sorely desire, And allow me to remember all That I acquire. And harm none so be it."*

The candle should be put down alongside your cauldron and allowed to burn out naturally.

## A Spell to Increase Personal Energy

You will need:

A few white candles - you need enough to create a circle around yourself

Some frankincense essential oil

Grape Seed oil

1 Magenta candle

Cast your circle as usual and then mix a drop of frankincense oil into some Grape Seed oil and anoint the candle with it.

Form a circle around yourself with the white candles.

Place the magenta candle in the middle, directly in front of you.

Light all the candles, starting at the top of the circle and working in a clockwise direction around. Finish off by light the magenta candle.

As you light the candles, chant,

*"Goddess of light and air, bring to me energy fair."*

Once all the candles have been lit, visualize their healing light streaming into you. Sit and meditate and, as you exhale, exhale all the stresses and strains of the day. As you inhale, breathe in the light and energy all around you.

Carry on until you feel that you have enough energy. If any of the candles are still burning, snuff them out one at a time.

# Chapter 13: Spells for Good Health

## Spells to Improve Health

As a Wiccan, you will often feel the need to cast healing spells for friends and family members. Before casting such a spell for others, do be sure that they would actually agree to having it done.

Most people will not have a problem with it but there are some who would be religiously opposed to it and it is not right to cast such spells without their consent or approval.

These healing spells should be done when the moon is waxing or when the moon is full. If possible, and the moon phase is right, do the spell on a Sunday.

If someone that you know is ill and you need them to get better in a hurry, but the time of the month or the day is wrong, don't stress about it – offer up a very simple prayer to the appropriate deity and mentally send light and love to the person who is ill. Visualize them getting better and being strong and well.

## A Healing Spell

Prepare beforehand by getting down to the specifics of what is necessary so that you can focus properly. Thinking, "Make Aunt Susie feel better." for example, is too generic. You should rather think something specific like "Shrink Aunt Susie's tumor."

You will need:

A blue candle

A fine paintbrush

A little watercolor paint in red

A little square of pure white paper

A little bowl of water - enough so that the paper can be submerged in it

Matches

A photo of the person being healed, if possible

Cast your circle as normal.

Light your candle as you chant, "I welcome you, Element of Water and Patron of Healing. Lend me your strength as I work in your name."

At the center of the white paper, paint an "X" using the brush and red watercolor, while chanting, "I name you - insert person's name- and then insert their problem."

Pick up the paper using both hands and hold it out in front of you. Visualize all the negative energy from the disease being drawn out by the symbol. That symbol must represent the person's illness.

Now submerge the paper in the water and swoosh it around a bit so that the watercolor smudges. At the same time chant, "I hereby wash away this pain's offence, be you gone and get you hence."

Keep swooshing around the paper and repeating the chant until the "X" is little more than a pale mark. Take the paper out of the water and crumple before tossing it out.

Take the bowl of water outside and pour it onto a clean piece of earth while saying, " And harm none so shall it be."

# Chapter 14: Spells for Attracting Love

## Spells to Bring You That Special Someone

It should be noted that Wiccan ethics prohibit us from forcing another person to love us through magic – we can, however, ask for love to be introduced into our lives. When writing spells for this purpose, think about the main attributes that you would like in a prospective partner and set them out accordingly. Do keep an open mind though – especially when it comes to characteristics that are not all that important to you.

## A Love Spell

A love spell should never be carried out with the intention of binding a particular person to yourself but you can ask for the love to be brought into your life. The best time for this spell is in the week following a new moon.

Red rose petals

3 yellow candles

1 white candle

One cup of mint tea

Cast the circle. Set out the yellow candles in a triangle directly in front of where you are sitting. The white candle goes in the center of this triangle. The rose petals should be scattered all around you.

Say the following:

"Venus, Goddess of Love, I invoke thee,

Venus, Goddess of Love, I invoke thee in order to bring me love,

Venus, Goddess of Love, I invoke thee to bring an end to my loneliness,

And harm none, so be it."

Drink the tea and then snub out each candle, one at a time, beginning with the white one.

Carefully pick up all the rose petals and lay them out on a tray to dry for 7 days. take them to a local river and scatter them.

## Finding Happiness in Love

Straight or votive candles in the following colors: one pink (friendship, spiritual healing), one light blue (inner peace, harmony, patience), and one gold (healing, happiness).

Lily of the valley oil

Saint-John's-Wort.

Jasmine or rose incense

Moss agate and amethyst tumbled stones

A small nail and a flower you like.

This spell should be cast on a Friday during a full moon or when the moon is waxing for best results.

Light the altar candles and the incense.

Using a nail, inscribe the word "love" on the pink candle, "peace" on the light blue one, and "success" on the gold candle.

Anoint the candles from the wick to the end.

Place the flower in the center of your altar; it should be a flower that in some manner represents happiness to you.

Set the candles in a triangular shape with the gold one at the top, the pink at the bottom left, and the light blue at the bottom right.

Place the agate between the gold and pink candles, and the amethyst between the gold and blue ones.

Light the gold candle first, then the others.

Say the chant three times.

Leave the candles to burn out completely.

Dispose of the wax afterward.

Chant "Open my life to happiness and joy. Fill my life with the wonder of peace and love. Open my eyes to the incoming happiness."

*Make me aware of all the good that comes into my life.*

# Chapter 15: Spells for Good Luck

## For Those Times When You Need Lady Luck on Your Side

### Protection Spell

For protection against negative people, you need:

A few drops of essential oil that correspond with your star sign

A picture of yourself

1 white candle

4 blue candles

3 black tourmaline stones

3 Acacia leaves

Sage incense

Start by washing your hands in a bowl of water that has a drop of your essential oil in it. Before casting the circle, put one blue candle at each cardinal point and place the white candle in front of you. The incense goes to the left of the white candle and the leaves and tourmaline stones go to the right of the candle. Your photo should be in front of the white candle.

Now cast your circle as normal and then light the candles and incense. Pass your photo over the incense three times whilst visualizing the incense purifying this representation of you and clearing away any negativity that has been sent your way by negative people.

Pick up the acacia leaves and black tourmaline and recite the following 5 times:

*"I invoke thee, Aradia, Goddess of protection and healing,*

*Protect me and keep me safe,*

*Now and forever.*

*And harm none, so be it.*

*Thank you."*

Visualize of protective aura of light surrounding you and your loved ones, one that nothing negative can penetrate. Put the candle out, close the circle, and let the incense burn itself out.

## Good Luck Spell

This is best done when the moon is waxing or when it is full.

3 candles –either gold or orange in color

Frankincense

A pen and piece of paper

Cast the circle and set the incense alight.

Visualize a triangle on the ground and place on candle at each point. Do not set them alight yet.

Say:

*"God and Goddess, Spirits and Guides*

*Thank you for what you have given me*

*I ask you to grant me [name what it is that you want]*

*Help me in my efforts to attain my goals*

*Please allow it to come to me at the right time*

*and harm none, so be it."*

Now spend some time imagining what it would be like if you had what you are asking for. Pay particular attention to the feelings associated with having your dream become a reality. Revel in the joy. Spend some time meditating on this and after a while, a symbol or image will come to you. When it does, draw it.

Now put that drawing inside the triangle you made with the candles.

Light one candle at a time, saying each time:

*"I call on fire to ignite my dream to the greatest good."*

Now stay still for a moment and visualize luck winging its way to you. Be certain in the knowledge that everything will happen for the best and be grateful for this. Be grateful for everything that you already have.

Now take your drawing and go outside and bury it, saying as you do so:

"I call on earth to bind my dream to the greatest good."

You may not get exactly what you ask for but you will get what is best for you. Be sure to watch for opportunities on the horizon.

## Change Your Luck

Straight or votive candles in the following colors: your astrological color, one orange (sudden change), one silver or light gray (neutralization of bad luck), one black (remove bad luck), and one magenta (to hurry the luck-changing process).

Lotus oil

Basil – fresh or dried

Frankincense or lotus incense

4 Pieces of carnelian or four clear quartz crystals.

Light the altar candles and the incense. Anoint the black candle from the end to the wick; the others from the wick to the end. Place the black candle in the center of your altar. Set your astrological candle in front of the black, with the other candles joining it in a circle around the central black candle. Place a stone beside each of these four candles.

Light the astrological candle and say: *"This is me and everything that represents me."*

Light the black candle and say: *"This is my bad luck. It now leaves me. I shed no tears over the parting."*

Light the silver candle and say: *"This neutralizes any remnants of bad luck. They dissolve into nothingness."*

Light the orange candle: *"This represents the changes for good that are coming into my life. I welcome them with open arms."*

Light the magenta candle: *"This is the astrological energy that I need to speed up the change."*

Sit for at least five minutes, repeating to yourself: "I *welcome change. I welcome the incoming good,* and harm none, so be it."

Do not allow any thoughts of failure or bad situations to enter your mind during this time.

Leave the candles to burn out completely. Dispose of the wax afterward.

Perform the spell during a full moon on a Thursday in order to change your luck.

## Find What is Lost

If you have lost something in your house, this quick and easy spell can help you to find it. With this one, you need not cast a circle, all you need is a white candle and the appropriate holder. Clear your mind for a minute or two in order to help you connect with the divine, light your candle and move from room to room while saying the following:

"Mother Goddess, hear my plea

open my eyes and help me to see"

Once you have found the item that you are looking for, be sure to snuff out the candle and thank the Goddess for her assistance.

## A Banishing Spell

This spell is useful when you have bad habits that you would like to rid yourself of in order to make yourself more productive. You can perform it on behalf of someone else, as long as you have their permission to do so.

Asking about whether or not you can perform a spell for someone in order to banish a bad habit can be a difficult conversation to have so it is best to leave this one alone, unless they ask you for help.

The aim here is to replace the bad behavior with good behavior - nature will always fill a vacuum so if you don't suggest a new behavior, you will find that the another, even worse behavior takes root.

You should conduct this spell when the moon is waning and, if possible, on a Saturday.

You will need:

1 Black Candle

The signature or hair of the person with the bad habit - your habit, if it's you.

A 2 inch square of pure white paper

1 Teaspoon of Epsom Salts

1 Teaspoon of pure alcohol

Matches

A Dish that is fire-proof

A pot of compost and a bulb

A mat that can withstand heat

Cast your circle as normal.

Light the candle as you chant, *"Wise one, Old one, Sure and Slow One, Guide this work and see it done."*

Take the hair or signature and hold it up while chanting, *"I name you (insert person's, or your, name)'s power."* Then wrap in the white paper square, and fold thrice.

Put the heat resistant bowl onto the mat and add the alcohol and Epsom Salts and set this mix on fire. With the paper in your hand chant, *"As the moon wanes to none, so shall your power be undone."*

Put the paper in the bowl and let it burn.

Pick up the bulb and, in front of the fire, chant, *"From the ashes I call the quality of (whatever quality you would have replace the one banished.)"*

Plant the bulb in the pot and, once the ashes from the fire have cooled off, add them as well.

The pot should be gifted to the person who the spell was about and cared for by them.

# Conclusion

Thank you again for downloading this book!

I hope that this gives you a great introduction to what it means to be a witch and I hope that this has inspired you to start your own quest.

What I find most wonderful about Wicca is that it is a spiritual path that is always growing – you will always be learning something new and so there is plenty to keep the voracious learners amongst us happy.

I hand over to you now and encourage you to begin your own journey and to start to learn more. I encourage you to read more on the subject online and to get started trying out the basic spells in this book.

In next to no time at all, you will build your confidence as a Wiccan and will be writing and casting your own spells.

Finally, if you enjoyed this book, please take the time to share your thoughts and post a review on Amazon. I would greatly appreciate it!

Yours in light and love – I speed you on your own spiritual quest.

Printed in Great Britain
by Amazon